The United Nations and
International Business

The United Nations and International Business

Sidney Dell

United Nations Institute for Training and Research
Duke University Press   Durham and London 1990

© 1990 United Nations Institute for Training and Research (UNITAR)
All rights reserved
Printed in the United States of America
on acid-free paper ∞
Library of Congress Cataloging-in-Publication Data
appear on the last printed page of this book.
UNITAR sales number E.89.III.K.RS/28

Contents

Foreword

A recent innovation in the program of the United Nations Institute for Training and Research (UNITAR) is the initiation of work on a history of the economic and social activities of the United Nations. Such histories exist for the International Monetary Fund and the World Bank and a number of books and articles have provided historical reviews of certain aspects of UN economic activities. But there is, thus far, no comprehensive account of the economic and social work of the United Nations constituting an institutional memory that could illuminate the many controversies that have arisen about international economic cooperation, and provide a source of reference for government officials and the academic community as well as for the interested public in general.

This monograph is a first step in filling the above need. It gives a historical account of some of the major activities of the United Nations that have implications for international business. There are many topics that could have been chosen as the starting point for the new UN history, and much could be said in favor of each of them. The selection of topic has been made with a view to throwing light on an area in which there has been much misunderstanding of UN objectives and motives, thus revealing a clear need to provide concerned readers with objective information that would enable them to judge the UN record in this field for themselves. The work has been supported by a special purpose grant from the Japanese government.

The text of this monograph will ultimately form part of the overall history of the economic and social activities of the United Nations when completed.

Michel Doo Kingué
United Nations Under-Secretary-General
and Executive Director of UNITAR

Introduction

There has been growing controversy in recent years about the relationship of the United Nations to international business. In the view of some observers, the United Nations has been guilty of antibusiness prejudice and, indeed, of decisions and actions hostile to the business community. Particular exception is often taken to UN activities having a bearing on the regulation of private business.

While the United Nations is not and should not be immune from criticism, it must be said that much of the criticism in this field is based on misunderstanding. Whatever the United Nations says or does with regard to international business reflects the collective decisions of its member governments—decisions that, in the economic as in other fields, are adopted increasingly by consensus. There is no United Nations other than the collectivity of member governments. Generally speaking, member governments regard themselves as representing domestic business along with other interests in the community. It is true that from time to time governments, both developed and developing, see the need for certain kinds of regulatory activity, and the business community itself has fully accepted this. Indeed, the many corporations that wish to maintain the highest standards of business conduct might have difficulty in doing so if others were not held to the same standards. It is, no doubt, partly for this reason that nongovernmental organizations representative of business, such as the International Chamber of Commerce, have cooperated actively in the work on a code of conduct on transnational corporations: while they certainly have views on what should and what should not be included in such a code, they have accepted the idea that a properly balanced code could help in improving relations between transnational corporations and the countries in which they operate.

It is also noteworthy that, as set out in the following pages, the very first activity of the United Nations concerning the regulation of international business was the result of an initiative by the U.S. administration under President Harry Truman, who could hardly be regarded as being hostile to the business community, national or international. Moreover, as noted in the latter sections of the study, the UN approach to international business has undergone a major shift of emphasis in recent years, in the sense of attaching more importance than hitherto to the potential role of transnational corporations as contributors to world development and to a safer and healthier world environment.

The author has benefited greatly from discussion of these and many other issues arising in this volume with numerous past and present members of the Secretariat and of delegations. Their help is gratefully acknowledged, especially since in many cases it would not otherwise have been possible to bring out the broad implications and inner realities underlying the publicly available documents. The author's thanks go particularly to Naoki Ishihara for his invaluable contributions to the entire project of which this book forms a part. He is greatly indebted also to the following, who were kind enough to read and comment upon portions of the text, and, in certain cases, supply drafts: Samuel Asante, Philippe Brusick, Bruce Harland, Iwona Rummel-Bulska, Sigmund Timberg, and Thomas Wälde.

Sidney Dell
December 1989

Abbreviations

ANDI	International Association of Industrialists
CCOL	Coordinating Committee for the Ozone Layer
CFCS	Chlorofluorocarbons
CTC	Centre on Transnational Corporations
DTCD	Department of Technical Cooperation for Development
EC	European Community
ECOSOC	Economic and Social Council
EEC	European Economic Community
FAO	Food and Agriculture Organization of the United Nations
G-77	Group of 77
GATT	General Agreement on Tariffs and Trade
ILO	International Labor Organization
ITO	International Trade Organization
NGO	nongovernmental organization
NIEO	New International Economic Order
OECD	Organization for Economic Cooperation and Development
RBP	restrictive business practices
TNC	transnational corporation
UNCTAD	UN Conference on Trade and Development
UNDP	UN Development Programme
UNEP	UN Environmental Programme
UNIDO	UN Industrial Development Organization
UNITAR	UN Institute for Training and Research
WHO	World Health Organization

1

International Efforts at Antitrust

The first UN initiative addressed directly to issues arising in the private business sector was the result of proposals by the United States, from 1945 onwards, for international action in the field of restrictive business practices (RBPS). Not until 1980 did it become possible for the United Nations to adopt a code of conduct on RBPS and in the intervening thirty-five years the matter was studied and restudied at the Havana Conference in 1947, in ECOSOC (Economic and Social Council), GATT (General Agreement on Tariffs and Trade), and UNCTAD (UN Conference on Trade and Development), as well as in some of the regional intergovernmental institutions such as the European Community and the OECD (Organization for Economic Cooperation and Development).

It should not occasion surprise that international agreements on complex political and economic issues often require lengthy periods of negotiation. National viewpoints on such issues usually differ widely, depending on the particular circumstances in which each country finds itself; and the policy positions of individual countries may change or fluctuate over time—sometimes in response to the course of the negotiations themselves.

Nowhere is this truer than in the field of RBPS. Even on the question of the propriety of action by international institutions to regulate the activities of private business, views differ from country to country, as well as changing radically over time in particular countries.

The issue is compounded where the subject of proposed regulation is RBPS. The entire philosophy and purpose of such regulation have been the subject of intense controversy at the national level over the past century. Questions have been raised not only regarding the effectiveness of government efforts to prevent or limit RBPs but also, more fundamentally, regarding the purposes to be served thereby.

In the United States, according to Galbraith: "The antitrust laws have been indiscriminately invoked against firms that have succeeded in building countervailing power, while holders of original market power, against whom the countervailing power was developed, have gone unchallenged. Such action has placed the authority of law on the side of positions of monopoly power and against the interests of the public at large."[1]

One of the most important instruments for exercise of countervailing power is the large retail organization, which is, according to Galbraith, "the public's main line of defense against the market power of those who produce or process consumers' goods." Despite this, the large retail organizations have been "not only a general, but also in some measure a unique object of government attack. . . . No explanation, however elaborate, can quite conceal the fact that the effect of antitrust enforcement, in this case, is to the disadvantage of the public."[2]

Similarly, though from a very different standpoint, Bork has suggested that "certain of [antitrust's] doctrines preserve competition, while others suppress it, resulting in a policy at war with itself."[3] Bork raises an even more fundamental point in arguing that since the ultimate purpose of antitrust legislation is to protect the welfare of the community, account must be taken of the manner in which restrictive practices affect welfare through productive efficiency. In his words:

> The integration of economic activities, which is indispensable to productive efficiency, always involves the implicit elimination of actual or potential competition. We allow it—indeed, should encourage it—because the integration creates wealth for the community. We should equally encourage those explicit and ancillary agreed-upon eliminations of rivalry that make the basic inte-

gration more efficient. To distinguish between the basic, implicit elimination of competition and the ancillary, explicit elimination would be a pointless contradiction in policy.[4]

Furthermore, Paul Samuelson has argued that: "Too often the law—as drawn up by Congress, enforced by the Department of Justice and adjudicated by the courts—regards various forms of competition that tend to eliminate firms and reduce the discrepancy between price and marginal cost as crimes rather than good deeds."[5]

Moreover, there is a sharp and unresolved conflict between opposing views of the criteria that should be applied in determining whether antitrust policy has been violated. Some lawyers and economists believe that the test should be whether a firm has "market power per se" stemming from its monopolistic market structure. Others consider that an updated "rule of reason" should apply, and that even the largest monopoly should be left undisturbed if it is dynamic, efficient, and innovative.[6]

A broader political consideration affecting public attitudes to the big corporations that have built positions of dominant market power for themselves has been pointed out by Richard Hofstadter: "The public is hardly unaware that the steepest rise in mass standards of living has occurred during the period in which the economy has been dominated by the big corporation."[7] And Hofstadter adds that for this reason the phrase "big business" no longer scares the public at large.[8]

It does not follow from the points made by Galbraith, Bork, Samuelson, and Hofstadter that national or international action to deal with RBPS is unwise or counterproductive. On the contrary, Bork himself asserts the need for legislation that strikes at the suppression of competition by horizontal agreement, including price-fixing and market-sharing; at horizontal mergers that create very large market shares; and at deliberate predation to drive out market rivals or prevent their entry.[9] And while Galbraith is skeptical about the effectiveness of antitrust legislation in "dispersing the economic power implicit in oligopoly,"[10] he recognizes that "the state must be expected to participate in the development of countervailing power"[11] and that this implies state interference with private decisionmaking, when necessary. There is, therefore, ample justification for efforts at both the national and international levels to prevent RBPS, though the determination of the best means for protecting the public interest in particular cases is not always straightforward and cannot in any case be based on simplistic criteria.

The Interwar Period

Attitudes to RBPS have changed considerably over the years. The regulation of such practices was first taken up internationally in the League of Nations after World War I.[12] During that period, the League published numerous reports and held frequent conferences on this subject, paying particular attention to international cartels and industrial agreements. In 1926, prior to the International Economic Conference of 1927 that took place in Geneva under League auspices, William Oualid published a study entitled *The Social Effects of International Industrial Agreements, The Protection of Workers and Consumers.*[13] Oualid perceived a large measure of international agreement on the question of regulation and supervision of cartels. The evidence he cited suggested that no country, not even the United States, was prohibiting cartels and RBPS outright. He proposed that the League should work toward a multilateral convention for the unification of national laws on RBPS and that all international industrial agreements in restraint of trade should be reported to, and recorded by, the League with a presumption of illegality attaching to any agreement not so filed. He further suggested the creation of institutional arrangements for investigation and enforcement, and the establishment of national and international procedures and sanctions against improper RBPS.

The Industrial Committee of the 1927 International Economic Conference declined to accept Oualid's recommendations on the grounds that the diversities in national attitudes were too great to permit the establishment of common norms and that many states objected to an international regime as contrary to the principles of national sovereignty and constitutional law.[14] The committee considered that the best way of mobilizing public support for action in this field and of discouraging abuses would be to give publicity to relevant developments, but it did not specify how this publicity was to be generated.

A number of other reports and memoranda on the cartel question were published by the League. These publications generally took a favorable attitude to cartels and industrial agreements while recognizing the possibility of abuse. The International Economic Conference's final report stated that:

> ... cartels and restrictive agreements could 'secure a more methodical organization of production and a reduction in costs by means of a better utilization of existing equipment, the development on more suitable lines of a new plant, and a more rational grouping of undertakings, and, on the other hand, act as a check on uneconomic competition and reduce the evils resulting from fluctuations in industrial activity. By this means they may assure to the workers greater stability of employment and at the same time, by reducing production and distribution costs and consequently selling prices, bring advantages to the consumer. . . . Nevertheless, the Conference considers . . . that such agreements, if they encourage monopolistic tendencies and the application of unsound business methods, may check technical progress in production and involve dangers to the legitimate interests of important sections of society and of particular countries.[15]

Subsequently, during the Great Depression, governmental attitudes veered even more strongly in favor of cartel agreements. A study submitted to the League of Nations in 1930 by a committee of experts concluded that certain specific international cartels had been wholly beneficial,[16] and by 1932 the League was viewing cartels as one of the best hopes for global economic recovery.[17] After some hesitation, the United States decided not to follow the European lead in fostering restrictive agreements as a means of dealing with the Depression.[18] The antitrust division of the Justice Department undertook a number of prosecutions and antitrust publicity in the late 1930s. In 1938 the U.S. Congress held hearings on economic concentration and made a substantial appropriation for studies in that field.

World War II provided a unique opportunity for extensive discovery of business accounts and other sources of information on the operations of cartels in pursuance of political and military objectives in Germany, Italy, and Japan. The intensity of feeling against cartels in the United States at the end of World War II is amply reflected in a book by Charles R. Whittlesey published in 1946. According to Whittlesey,

> To most Americans, cartels are an alien, and more especially a German institution. They have incurred the special antipathy which the war aroused toward all things German and non-democratic. The use made of cartel connections to promote German military and political designs and the charge that American businesses were duped in the process further added to their disrepute, as did the fact that cartels were made the instrument for extending German control over the economic life of occupied countries.[19]

These perceptions helped to reverse, at any rate in the United States, the thinking of the Depression period regarding the beneficent nature of restrictive agreements. Apart from this it was natural that the United States, in the strong economic position in which it found itself at the end of World War II, should be concerned to promote a more liberal framework for the world economy and the greatest possible dismantling of the trade and exchange restrictions that had caused havoc during the Great Depression by aggravating the collapse of world trade.

Postwar National and International Action

The process began during the military occupation of Germany and Japan after the war. Steps were taken toward the adoption of antitrust measures for these countries, based on the U.S. model, in the hope that this would contribute toward ensuring that the industrial powers of these countries would be used only for peaceful and domestic purposes. Despite the fact that antitrust policies had been imposed by the occupying powers, after the end of the occupation the federal German courts continued to recognize as precedents the antitrust decisions handed down during the occupation. Ultimately a law against restraint of competition was passed in 1957 which adopted the Sherman Act approach of prohibiting trade restraints. While the law provided for a considerable number of exemptions, it departed from the general European tradition of condemning only those trade restraints found to be against the public interest or constituting abuses of market power. Japan adopted a similar strategy, though this was subsequently weakened by exempting amendments.

Other countries also introduced antitrust measures such as the U.K. Restrictive Trade Practices and Monopoly Act of 1948, the Swedish law of 1952, and the Laniel Decree of 1953 in France. The establishment of the European Economic Community (EEC) was a particularly important stimulus to national antitrust legislation because the Rome Treaty contained in Articles 85 to 90 important provisions prohibiting restrictive business practices affecting intra-EEC trade. European antitrust laws, unlike the Sherman Act, were not the result of a condemnation of cartels in principle, but were rather an expression of public policy. Thus, for example, Article 86 of the Rome Treaty recognized that dominant enterprises might abuse their market positions, and imposed legal liability in the event of such abuse. But there was nothing in the European legislation comparable to Section 7 of the U.S. Clayton Act, which prohibited mergers having a probable tendency to lessen competition, or Section 2 of the Sherman Act attacking monopolies. Similarly, in the United States price fixing, territorial allocation, and production-limiting agreements among competitors were illegal per se and could not be justified by any economic consideration. This was not the case under the European antitrust laws, which permitted the authorities to decide whether such agreements were contrary to the public interest.[20]

Attitudes were, however, subject to change over time. In the process of enforcing the Rome Treaty, the Commission of the

European Community tended to strengthen the resistance of the EEC as a whole to anticompetitive practices. On the other hand, changes in the membership of the U.S. Supreme Court led, during the 1970s and 1980s, to a more laissez-faire approach to the activities of U.S. private enterprise than had prevailed in previous years: in the antitrust area the Court tended to avoid presumptions of per se illegality in favor of a "rule of reason" test that frequently favored business defendants.

The ITO Phase

In December 1945 the United States circulated to governments for their consideration a document entitled *Proposals for Expansion of World Trade and Employment.* These proposals advocated the establishment of an International Trade Organization (ITO), the members of which would agree to conduct their commercial relations in accordance with rules to be set forth in the charter of the organization.

Chapter V of the draft U.S. charter dealt with RBPs.[21] Members were to agree to act individually and collectively to prevent business practices that would restrain competition, restrict access to markets, or foster monopolistic control in international trade.

Among the practices to be covered by the above provision were combinations, agreements, or other arrangements which

(a) fixed prices or the terms or conditions of purchase or sale of any product or service;
(b) excluded enterprises from any territorial market or fields of business activity, allocated or divided markets or fields of business activity, allocated customers, or fixed sales or purchase quotas, subject to certain exceptions;
(c) boycotted or discriminated against particular enterprises;
(d) limited production or fixed production quotas;
(e) suppressed technology or invention;
(f) extended the use of rights under patents, trademarks, or copyrights in an unauthorized manner.

Provision was to be made for a complaints procedure, and for appropriate remedial measures to be implemented by member countries in accordance with their respective laws and procedures. The organization was to be empowered to prepare and publish reports concerning such complaints and arrange consultative conferences among individual members as necessary. It was also to be authorized to request information from members and conduct appropriate studies.

Member countries were to undertake to transmit information requested by the organization and carry out such investigations as might be necessary for this purpose. They were also to take action, after recommendation by the organization, to terminate particular RBPs in accordance with each member's system of law and economic organization.

There were to be certain exceptions to the provisions set out in chapter V, notably with respect to intergovernmental commodity agreements meeting the requirements of chapter VI of the charter.

Clearly, these were proposals of a very far-reaching character. In retrospect it may be said that they implied a degree of commitment by member governments to the decisions of an international organization that has not in fact been found practicable, not only in the area of RBPs but in any other area of international action in the economic field.

The Proposed Mandate for ITO

In October 1946 a preparatory committee met in London to prepare the way for the projected UN Conference on Trade and Employment. The report of the first session of that committee contains a summary of the positions taken by governments with regard to the above-mentioned U.S. proposals.[22]

The report summed up the discussion as follows:

In preliminary exchanges of views it was found on the one hand that some delegates regarded these practices as invariable and automatic barriers to a free and expanding system of international trade and in conflict with the obligations which it was proposed members of the Organization would assume under other chapters of the Charter. On the other hand some delegates perceived considerable advantages in their wise use, particularly in introducing stability in industries requiring large investment and depending mainly on external markets. It was also urged that restrictive agreements were frequently accompanied by exchanges of technical information which facilitated establishment of new industries in the less industrialized countries.

It was found, however, that, despite this wide divergence of view on the significance of these practices, there was a unanimous belief that they were capable of having harmful effects on the expansion of production and trade and the maintenance in all countries of high levels of real income and on the other purposes of the Organization, whether, as some felt, by their very nature, or as others maintained, only in their wrongful use. Accordingly it was agreed that all members of the Organization should undertake to take all possible steps within their jurisdiction to prevent restrictive practices having harmful effects on the purposes of the Organization.[23]

The Preparatory Committee was in agreement that the ITO should be empowered to receive complaints and to investigate them. "It was felt," said the Preparatory Committee, "that this was the most important function which the Organization could discharge in this field."[24] It was also felt that ITO should undertake studies and arrange conferences in the field of RBPS.

The points of view expressed in the Preparatory Committee were subsequently repeated at the Havana Conference itself. Some countries would have wished to place even greater limitations on the responsibilities of ITO than were implied in the report of the Preparatory Committee. For example, exception was taken by some countries to the inclusion of anything in the charter that might appear similar to a judicial procedure, and a proposal was made that the word "complaints" should not be used but rather the word "claims." A number of developing countries pressed for recognition in the ITO Charter of the legitimacy of the activities of government agencies that were designed primarily to stabilize domestic prices.

In the light of the discussion that had taken place both in London and Havana, the following compromise between divergent views was adopted in chapter V of the ITO Charter: "Each Member shall take appropriate measures and shall cooperate with the Organization to prevent, on the part of private or public commercial enterprises, business practices affecting international trade which restrain competition, limit access to markets, or foster monopolistic control, whenever such practices have harmful effects on the expansion of production or trade and interfere with the achievement of any of the other objectives set forth in Art. 1."[25]

In pursuance of the above, provision was made for a complaints procedure as well as for consultation and investigation, as appropriate. It was also laid down that special procedures were required in respect of RBPs in relation to certain services.

For the purposes of the ITO Charter, RBPs were defined as including the following:

(a) fixing prices, terms or conditions to be observed in dealing with others in the purchase, sale or lease of any product;
(b) excluding enterprises from, or allocating or dividing, any territorial market or field of business activity, or allocating customers, or fixing sales quotas or purchase quotas;
(c) discriminating against particular enterprises;
(d) limiting production or fixing production quotas;
(e) preventing by agreement the development or application of technology or invention whether patented or unpatented;
(f) extending the use of rights under patents, trademarks or copyrights granted by any Member to matters which, according to its laws and regulations, are not within the scope of such grants, or to products or conditions of production, use or sale which are likewise not the subjects of such grants;

(g) any similar practices which the Organization may declare, by a majority of two-thirds of the Members present and voting, to be restrictive business practices.[26]

It will be seen that the definition of RBPs adopted at Havana conformed fairly closely to that which had been proposed by the United States in its suggested charter, referred to above. The most important departure from the U.S. proposals was that ITO action was to be limited to RBPs having "harmful effects on the expansion of production or trade," as indicated in the above-mentioned article.

In addition, the burden of responsibility for determining whether action by ITO was called for was shifted in a crucial respect. Under the U.S. suggested charter any of the practices listed under the definition of RBPs were to be presumed as having harmful effects calling for appropriate action "unless shown to the contrary in a specific case." In the ITO Charter, on the other hand, appropriate measures were called for only where the practices in question had harmful effects on the expansion of production or trade, and this made it necessary for ITO to make a determination in each instance as to whether a practice was having or was about to have the "harmful effects" mentioned in Article 46.1.

The "harmful effects" limitation was responsive in part to the position taken by developing countries on the activities of public commercial enterprises engaged in stabilization activities: such activities would come into conflict with the charter only if they had "harmful effects on the expansion of production or trade."

Efforts in ECOSOC

Congressional opposition to the ITO Charter led, late in 1950, to withdrawal of the U.S. administration's request for ratification. The U.S. government continued to believe, however, that there was a need for regulation of international restraints on trade and decided to place chapter V of the ITO

Charter before ECOSOC as an independent issue. This decision coincided with a request by Congress to the administration to intensify its anti-cartel activity in foreign countries.[27]

In arguing for action by ECOSOC in 1951, the U.S. representative suggested that although many of the pre-World War II cartels had ceased to exist, or had been weakened, there were signs of their resurgence, which, if it occurred, would undo much of the positive work of GATT, the European Payments Union, and the Schuman Plan. There were, he said, four types of abuse that were characteristic of cartels:

1. Markets were allocated to suppliers on the basis of geographical areas and export quotas, thereby not only hindering the growth of trade but also frustrating the efforts of underdeveloped countries to promote particular export industries.

2. "Varied and ruthless" measures were adopted to limit investment in productive facilities in countries regarded as export markets, and to deny access to patents and technical knowledge, as well as to credit and the supply of raw materials. If such measures failed to achieve their purpose, cartel members had been known to acquire shares in locally owned plants "not for the purpose of developing them, but for the purpose of retarding and limiting their growth."

3. By restricting competition, cartel arrangements also restricted production and employment.

4. Cartels impaired productivity by protecting inefficient companies, preventing full capacity operation in low-cost plants, and, through restrictive agreements, delaying the introduction of new technologies and more efficient methods of production.

The U.S. representative did not deal with cases in which single corporations might be in a position to adopt restrictive practices on the above lines.

The United States suggested that member states should cooperate with one another to prevent restraints on competition, the limitation of access to markets, or the fostering of monopolistic control whenever such practices would have harmful effects on the expansion of production or trade, on the economic development of underdeveloped areas or on standards of living. Since many of the arrangements restricting trade extended beyond the jurisdiction of any one country, international collaboration was necessary in order that effective action might be taken.

The U.S. proposal received considerable support in ECOSOC, though generally with some qualifications. The Western European attitude, as reflected particularly in statements by representatives of Belgium, France, and Sweden, was less hostile to cartels than that of the United States. The French representative thought there were good as well as bad intercompany agreements. For example, international agreements might make it possible to pool high cost research and the use of large-scale installations that were beyond the capabilities of single firms or the absorptive capacity of single markets. The dividing up of export markets in such cases as that of the motor vehicle industry made it possible for exporters to compete abroad who would not otherwise have been able to do so because of inability to incur the costs of maintaining adequate supplies of spare parts in all markets. Attitudes to such problems were conditioned by differences in the size of markets: international agreements between companies meant one thing in the unified continents and something quite different in the old continent of Europe. The Western European countries nevertheless favored greater supervision of harmful restrictive practices.

Among developing countries, Chile, India, Mexico, and Uruguay pointed out that government or state monopolies were essential to the development of their countries and the protection of the interests of the general public. The Mexican representative said that while his government favored measures to promote world trade and production, it was also aiming at a certain degree of self-sufficiency for the country. The Uruguayan representative suggested that any measures proposed for adoption should be based on the principles set forth in chapter V of the Havana Charter, which drew a distinction between acceptable and harmful monopolies from the point of view of whether they served the general interests of the population.

The representatives of Czechoslovakia, Poland, and the USSR said that the U.S. proposal was designed to camouflage the objectives of U.S. monopolies which were seeking to dominate world markets, exploit underdeveloped countries, and discriminate against the socialist countries. The U.S. representative denied these allegations, and said that the socialist countries were themselves responsible for the deterioration in trade relations.

In the event ECOSOC, basing itself on the U.S. proposal (with minor amendments), decided by 12 votes to 3 with 2 abstentions to recommend to member states that they take "appropriate" measures "to prevent, on the part of private or public commercial enterprises, business practices affecting international trade which restrain competition, limit access to markets or foster monopolistic control, whenever such practices have harmful effects on the expansion of production or trade, on the economic development of underdeveloped areas or on standards of living." These measures, said the council, should be based on the principles set forth in chapter V of the Havana Charter concerning restrictive business practices. In addition, the council established a ten-member ad hoc committee on restrictive business practices which was instructed to make proposals, not later than March 1953, for implementing the recommendation referred to above. To this end the ad hoc committee was to obtain and analyze information from both public and private sources on restrictive business practices and on legislation adopted by member states with the object of "restoring the freedom of competition." The Secretary-General was requested to explore the views of intergovernmental bodies "as to the organization which could most appropriately implement these proposals" (Economic and Social Council Resolution 375 (XIII) of September 13, 1951).

The report of the ad hoc committee (E/2380) was duly submitted to the Economic and Social Council (ECOSOC) at its sixteenth session, held from June 30 to August 5, 1953. The committee presented twenty draft articles of a proposed international agreement, covering both the substantive principles and procedures for an international organization that would be given responsibility for preventing and controlling restrictive business practices on the basis of the principles set out in chapter V of the Havana Charter. The committee also defined the conditions under which restrictive business practices might be subject to investigation by the organization, and the obligations of governments in carrying out the organization's purposes. The report that had been requested from the Secretary-General regarding the organization that should assume the above responsibilities was not in fact submitted because there had been insufficient time to consult the GATT Contracting Parties.

The committee also transmitted to the council a report by the committee's secretary (E/2379 and Add. 1) analyzing government measures in the field of restrictive business practices.

The council had a preliminary round of discussion of the committee's report, but many members felt that governments should be given more time to consider the issues that had been raised. This would have the advantage of allowing the Secretary-General to fulfil his mandate under the council's previous resolution. Some representatives, particularly the representative of Belgium, cautioned against the idea that restrictive business practices always had harmful effects: it was suggested that cartels and combines could help in introducing greater flexibility into the economy as well as making it possible to regulate economic development and hence provide for stability of employment. They could also direct capital into the most productive channels. Belgium, Sweden, and other countries stressed the need for prevention and control of governmental as well as private restrictions on trade.

The council decided by 16 votes to 0 with 2 abstentions (Resolution 487 (XVI) of July 31, 1953) to have the committee's report transmitted to member states and specialized agencies for examination and comment, and it requested the Secretary-General to circulate any comments received, together with such analysis as he might consider appropriate, and to submit the report that had been requested of him at the thirteenth session. The council decided further to take up the question again in 1955 at its nineteenth session.

At the 1955 session a number of new papers were presented,

notably the comments that had been requested from governments and specialized agencies, a report on current legal developments in the field of restrictive business practices and a report on restrictive business practices in international trade, dealing with ten industries.

Council views were divided on the draft articles of agreement previously proposed by the ad hoc committee. Some countries supported the draft agreement but others felt it would be better to make a start with a regional rather than a universal approach to the subject. It was pointed out that there were great disparities in national legislation in this field, so that the agreement would impose unequal burdens on the various countries: the first step should, therefore, be to bring the various national laws to a uniform level. A number of proposals were made regarding the organization that should assume the responsibilities envisaged in the draft articles, but the consensus was that the time was not yet ripe for the adoption of the draft agreement. On May 26, 1955, therefore, the council adopted by 14 votes to 0 with 3 abstentions Resolution 568(XIX) in which it reaffirmed its continuing concern with the existence in international trade of harmful restrictive business practices and requested the Secretary-General to continue circulating information on this subject and to suggest further consideration of the matter "at a later session of the Council."

It is of interest that the United States—the country that had taken initiatives in 1945 and 1951 with a view to the international regulation of RBPs through an appropriate international institution—had by 1955 become convinced that under existing conditions such a step might actually be counterproductive.[28] In a press release issued on March 28, 1955, the U.S. government pointed out that

in order to recommend action against cartel practices, the proposed international body would be required not only to find that such practices exist, but that they have harmful effects on production or trade in the light of very general criteria. This latter determination would be extremely difficult for a body of governmental representatives to make in the light of the substantial divergencies in approach previously referred to, and, in the opinion of the United States Government, would likely result in the condoning of restrictive practices or in no agreement by the international body on the disposition of complaints brought before it.

In addition, since action under the proposed agreement would be primarily a matter of enforcement procedures under national laws, the present stage of development of national legislation offers little hope that recommendations of the international body could be effectively carried out. While encouraged by the progress which has been made in recent years in this field, the United States does not feel that the point has been reached at which a broad international arrangement of the type proposed by the Committee could be successfully implemented. (*The Department of State Bulletin,* April 18, 1955, p. 665)

The United States, therefore, came to the conclusion that what was needed for the time being was not new machinery but the further development and harmonization of national programs to deal with restrictive business practices.

The draft agreement did get the general support of seven countries that were not without influence in the matter.[29] But without the endorsement of the country that had taken the lead in this field in the past, ECOSOC felt that it would be best to defer further consideration of the subject, and in the meantime provide for an exchange of information through the Secretary-General, as noted above.

In taking the position set out above, the U.S. government implicitly rejected the arguments advanced by the secretary of the ad hoc committee, Sigmund Timberg, who was and is himself an American lawyer of distinction. In his view ". . . national efforts to counteract the activities of international cartels and combines are largely ineffective because of territorial limitations. Hence, not taking action against restrictive business practices in international trade is tantamount to abandoning the prospect of action against most such practices."[30]

Timberg did not deny that the need to prove "harmful effects" would render the proposed UN agreement a much weaker instrument than the U.S. Sherman Act. But this did not mean that U.S. interests would suffer any more than they already did under existing conditions. As matters stood, U.S. enterprises were already at a disadvantage through being subject to the strict regime of the Sherman Act, while the enterprises of other countries were not. The proposed agreement would not reduce the obligations of U.S. enterprises under the Sherman Act, and its impact on the enterprises of other countries could only be to raise the levels of antitrust enforcement abroad, thereby reducing the degree of discrimination against the former.[31]

The GATT Phase

In connection with the review of the General Agreement on Tariffs and Trade undertaken at the ninth session of the Contracting Parties in 1955, proposals were made by the delegations of Denmark, Norway, and Sweden and by the Federal Republic of Germany to include in the agreement provisions along the lines of chapter V of the Havana Charter, dealing with RBPS. However, since ECOSOC had not yet completed its action on the matter, it was decided to postpone consideration in GATT to the next regular session of the Contracting Parties. The question was taken up again at the twelfth session of the Contracting Parties in October–November 1957. The GATT secretariat was instructed to collect and analyze all the available material concerning any intergovernmental agreements that had been proposed or prepared with a view to preventing or checking the harmful effects of RBPS in international trade. For this task the Executive Secretary engaged Professor J. L'Huillier of the University of Geneva. The memorandum prepared by Professor J. L'Huillier was published in a booklet entitled *Restrictive Trade Practices.*

At their thirteenth session in November 1958 the Contracting Parties decided to appoint a group of governmental experts to study and make recommendations "with regard to whether, to what extent if at all, and how the Contracting Parties should undertake to deal with restrictive business practices in international trade."[32] The group of experts duly submitted their report, which was adopted by the Contracting Parties on June 2, 1960. Subsequently, on November 18, 1960, the Contracting Parties adopted a decision[33] on arrangements for consultations regarding RBPS. The decision contained several noteworthy elements. It recognized the need for international cooperation "to deal effectively with harmful restrictive practices in international trade." It stated, however, that "in present circumstances it would not be practicable for the Contracting Parties to undertake any form of control of such practices nor to provide for investigations." It provided, therefore, for a procedure whereby "at the request of any contracting party a contracting party should enter into consultations on such practices on a bilateral or multilateral basis as appropriate." At the conclusion of each such consultation the requesting party and the party addressed were invited to inform the GATT secretariat of the nature of the complaint and of the conclusion reached, whether mutually satisfactory or otherwise. The GATT secretariat was instructed to convey this information to the Contracting Parties.

Thus, the ambitious ideas for comprehensive control of cartels that had originated in the United States and been reflected in the Havana Charter had not survived the efforts made over a period of fourteen years to implement them in ECOSOC and GATT. All that was left, for the time being, was a mild invitation to governments to consult on the means for avoiding the harmful effects of international business restraints whenever they felt sufficiently disturbed by such restraints to do so. It appears, in fact, that no specific cases of consultation under the above procedure was ever reported to the GATT secretariat, and no further action with regard to RBPS was taken by the Contracting Parties.

In 1986, however, a case was brought before GATT alleging that the world market for copper ores and concentrates had been adversely affected by RBPS in Japan. Following a request by the European Community for the establishment of a working party, the GATT Council decided on July 15, 1986, to set up the group of governmental experts on measures affecting the world market for copper ores and concentrates. The terms of reference of the group were as follows: "To examine problems falling under the competence of the General Agreement relating to current trends in world trade in copper, including the supply and demand situation for copper concentrates and refined copper, and to report to the Council."

It was argued in the group that current shortages in copper concentrates were a result of the fact that custom smelters in Japan had been able to offer higher prices for copper concentrates as a result of government and other policies, such as tariff protection of domestic refined copper production, higher domestic prices of refined copper compared with market prices, and unofficial import quotas. It was suggested further that abnormally high internal prices for copper metal in Japan were possible only on the basis of concealed import restrictions which were in violation of several provisions of GATT.

In reply Japan contended that the tariffs maintained on copper products were fully legitimate under GATT and that the terms and conditions of purchasing contracts were outside the competence of GATT, being determined purely by commercial considerations. Prices for refined copper were based on free competition; and there was no government intervention in prices, no price cartel, nor had any restrictions been imposed on imports of refined copper. Neither was there any evidence of hidden restrictive practices in trade or pricing policy in Japan.

No agreement was reached within the group as to whether the above-mentioned pricing and trading practices constituted a distortion in the supply and demand situation of copper concentrates, with an aggravating impact on world trade conditions. The hope was expressed that further liberalization of copper trade would be achieved through the Uruguay Round of trade negotiations.

During preparations for the Uruguay Round, ten developing countries[34] initially proposed that RBPs be made a subject of negotiations. This proposal was not, however, pursued and the issue was not mentioned in the Punta del Este declaration.

The Work of UNCTAD

After the successive failures of ECOSOC and GATT to deal decisively with the question of restrictive business practices there was an interval of some years in which no further action was taken within the UN framework. In 1968, however, at the second conference of UNCTAD the question came up for consideration once again. On this occasion the stimulus came from developing countries, which were concerned about the effects of RBPS on the development process and particularly on their exports. Following an initiative of Brazil, which received the support of the Group of 77 (G-77), the conference decided: "that a study be carried out on the question of the restrictive business practices adopted by private enterprises of developed countries, with special references to the effects of such practices on the export interests of the developing countries, especially on the relatively least developed."[35]

The resolution was adopted by 57 votes to 12 with 9 abstentions. The OECD countries, however, objected to a study limited to RBPS by private enterprises of developed countries. This important controversy was finally resolved at UNCTAD IV in Nairobi in 1976, when it was agreed that the RBPS to be studied were those adversely affecting international trade, particularly the trade and development of developing countries. This formulation made it clear that the studies should cover all firms, including those that were state owned, and that they should not be limited to RBPS affecting developing countries but should cover all countries.

The study requested by the conference was completed in 1971, providing the basis for action at the third session of the conference in 1972. At that session, the conference adopted—this time without dissent—a resolution recognizing "that work being done on Restrictive Business Practices constitutes an important component of the programme of work on the liberalization of barriers to the trade of developing countries in manufactures and semi-manufactures."[36]

The conference decided to establish an ad hoc group of experts on RBPS, consisting of "an adequate number of governmental and non-governmental experts to be nominated by the

Secretary-General of UNCTAD after consultations with Governments." The tasks of the group were to include:

(a) The identification of all RBPs, with a view to submission of recommendations for alleviating and, where possible, eliminating such practices.
(b) Further study of RBPs that had already been identified, such as those resulting from cartel activities, export prohibitions, agreements on market sharing, tied purchasing, restrictions on transfer of technology, and arbitrary transfer pricing.
(c) Greater attention than in the past to RBPs connected with licensing arrangements, patents and trademarks, market sharing, pricing policy, and participation of firms of developing countries in industrial projects of multinational corporations.

The group was also to examine the possibility of drawing up, for the consideration of all governments, guidelines on RBPs adversely affecting developing countries.

Following initial work on the question of guidelines, UNCTAD's Committee on Manufactures decided at its seventh session in June/July 1975 to convene a second ad hoc group of experts on RBPs. This group held two sessions, in October 1975 and March 1976, and, among other things, agreed on an extensive list of "RBPs affecting international trade."[37]

This made it possible for UNCTAD IV, held in Nairobi in 1976, to launch negotiations having the objective: ". . . of formulating a set of multilaterally agreed equitable principles and rules for the control of restrictive business practices having adverse effects on international trade, particularly that of developing countries, and on the economic development of these countries."[38] This resolution represented a significant advance on the "guidelines" previously envisaged.[39]

Preparatory work for the above-mentioned negotiations was entrusted to a third ad hoc group of experts on RBPs. The group held six sessions from 1976 to 1978, and by the end of its sixth session had made sufficient progress to create a basis for the final negotiations. Accordingly, in September 1978 the Trade and Development Board was able to recommend to the UN General Assembly the convening of a conference on RBPS to complete the "Set of Principles and Rules."

The UN Conference on Restrictive Business Practices

The General Assembly, in resolution 33/155, decided to convene the conference in the last quarter of 1979 and authorized UNCTAD V, which was to be held in Manila, to complete the preparatory work, including the adoption of decisions on the issues for discussion. The RBP Conference took place in two sessions, held from November 19–December 7, 1979, and April 8–18, 1980, respectively, and was successful in reaching agreement by consensus on a "Set of Principles and Rules." As Professor Dale A. Oesterle has pointed out, this was "the first global negotiation to produce a compact on the control of restrictive business practices since formal international discussions on the issue began over fifty years ago."[40]
The main issues before the conference were the following:

(a) the extent to which the code would be a mandatory or voluntary instrument;
(b) the extent to which special or differential treatment should be accorded to developing countries;
(c) the extent to which the rules should contain escape clauses permitting the use of particular practices in particular cases;
(d) the extent to which export and international cartels should be controlled;
(e) the extent to which intra-firm behavior and transactions of transnational corporations should be covered; and
(f) the extent to which the "Set of Principles and Rules" should apply to state-owned or mixed enterprises, as well as to private enterprises.[41]

Discussion on the legal status of the code—the first of the above issues—was similar to that which was taking place concurrently in connection with the negotiations for a code of conduct on transnational corporations (TNCs). Developing and socialist countries favored a mandatory instrument, while the OECD countries felt that they could not go beyond a voluntary code. A consensus was, therefore, reached to transmit the text of the "Set of Principles and Rules" (referred to subsequently as the Set) to the General Assembly for adoption as a resolution. This the General Assembly did at its thirty-fifth session in Resolution 35/63 of December 5, 1980. Since the resolution was adopted by consensus, without a vote, and without the expression of any reservations by any delegation after the adoption, it represented a fairly strong commitment on the part of all member countries present, though not as strong a commitment as a treaty or convention subject to ratification.

One question that is not dealt with explicitly in the Set is that of the extra-territorial application of national RBP legislation. As Brusick points out: "Where an export cartel is authorized and registered under national restrictive business practice legislation in one country, it is difficult to take action against it in the country which is affected without opening the question of national sovereignty and extra-territorial application of national laws."[42]

The Set does, however, call for states and enterprises to avoid agreements or practices that would adversely affect international trade, and particularly the trade and development of developing countries. For example, it calls on enterprises not to adopt agreements for fixing prices, including the prices of exports and imports, and it urges states to seek appropriate measures to prevent and/or control RBPs within their competence whenever they are likely to have such adverse effects.[43]

Negotiation of the Set encountered the same problems with regard to applicability to state-owned enterprises as did the negotiations for a code of conduct on TNCs. The problem arose as a result of the contention of the socialist countries that state-owned enterprises cannot be regarded as TNCs, and do not engage in RBPs because of the legal, social, and economic conditions prevailing in these countries. All countries other than socialist countries, however, considered that state-owned enterprises should be subject to the same disciplines as private firms, whether in the context of measures to deal with RBPs or of the code of conduct on TNCs. In the end, it was agreed that the Set applies to all enterprises (Section B, paras. 6, 7) and that the word "enterprises" includes all forms of legal associations "irrespective of the mode of creation or control or ownership, private or State, which are engaged in commercial activities" (Section B, para. 3). A similar approach has been adopted in the negotiations on a code of conduct on TNCs, as indicated in the discussion of this subject in chapter 4.

The Content of the Set of Principles and Rules

The objectives of the Set are as follows:

1. To ensure that restrictive business practices do not impede or negate the realization of benefits that should arise from the liberalization of tariff and non-tariff barriers affecting world trade, particularly those affecting the trade and development of developing countries;
2. To attain greater efficiency in international trade and development, particularly that of developing countries, in accordance with national aims of economic and social development and existing economic structures, such as through:
(a) the creation, encouragement and protection of competition;
(b) control of the concentration of capital and/or economic power;
(c) encouragement of innovation;
3. To protect and promote social welfare in general and, in particular, the interests of consumers in both developed and developing countries;
4. To eliminate the disadvantages to trade and development which may result from the restrictive business practices of transnational corporations or other enterprises, and thus help to maximize benefits to international trade and particularly the trade and development of developing countries;
5. To provide a set of multilaterally agreed equitable prin-

ciples and rules for the control of restrictive business practices for adoption at the international level and thereby to
facilitate the adoption and strengthening of laws and policies in this area at the national and regional levels.

The Set defines restrictive business practices as "acts or behaviour of enterprises which, through an abuse or acquisition
and abuse of a dominant position of market power, limit access
to markets or otherwise unduly restrain competition, having
or being likely to have adverse effects on international trade,
particularly that of developing countries, and on the economic
development of these countries, or which through formal, informal, written or unwritten agreements or arrangements
among enterprises have the same impact."

The term "dominant position of market power" is defined
as a situation "where an enterprise, either by itself or acting
together with a few other enterprises, is in a position to control
the relevant market for a particular good or service or group of
goods or services." Oesterle points out that this wording leaves
it unclear whether it includes shared monopoly, tacit collusion,
or conscious parallelism—all much-debated concepts in U.S.
antitrust law. This, as well as the basic Set definition of RBPs,
reflected a compromise following difficult negotiations, and
further negotiations would be required if it were decided that
the existing definitions need to be refined. As regards scope of
application, while the Set covers all transactions in goods and
services that affect international trade adversely, particularly
the trade of developing countries, it does not apply to intergovernmental agreements such as commodity agreements, nor
does it cover RBPs that are the outcome of such agreements.

The Set calls on enterprises including TNCs to conform to
the laws governing RBPs in the countries in which they operate.
Where national legislation goes beyond the Set in proscribing
certain practices, such legislation prevails. The Set also states
that, in the event of proceedings under national laws, enterprises should be subject to the jurisdiction of the national courts
and relevant administrative bodies. This contrasts with the negotiations on the code of conduct on TNCs in which home coun-

tries have urged recognition of the applicability of international law and the possibility of recourse to proceedings outside local courts, such as international arbitration. This difference presumably arises from the fact that the scope of the Set does not include questions concerning the nationalization of TNC property and that RBPs are not covered by customary international law.

The Set specifies the particular practices that should be avoided by enterprises and indicates the manner in which a judgment should be made as to whether particular acts or behavior should be regarded as abusive and therefore governed by the Set. Particularly noteworthy is the fact that vertical restraints of enterprises in a dominant position of market power are covered. In other words, the Set calls for avoidance of RBPs by enterprises in a dominant position of market power over other enterprises at a different level of the distribution chain. Brusick suggests that this provision of the Set has the merit that it goes further than any existing national legislation. As he points out:

> In the European Economic Community, vertical arrangements between manufacturers and distributors restricting the free flow of goods within the Common Market are subject to Articles 85 and 86 of the Treaty of Rome. However, where vertical arrangements affect trade with third countries only, no such prohibition applies. In the United States, with the exception of resale price maintenance, which is *per se* prohibited, vertical restraints at present are only challenged if they have horizontal effects.[44]

On the other hand, Oesterle argues that in certain respects the Set is more lenient than U.S. law on vertical agreements, discriminatory pricing, and mergers. Moreover the Set does not permit conclusive presumptions or per se rules regarding business agreements, which form an important part of U.S. antitrust jurisprudence. Under Set business agreements have to be scrutinized and all the facts gathered and evaluated to permit a judgment to be made as to whether they are anticompetitive.

It is, of course, not surprising that there are divergences between the provisions of Set and those of the corresponding national legislation of particular countries. The existence of such divergences is less important than the fact that a common basis was agreed among all the participating countries. As noted earlier, it was the conflict between national views and legislation regarding RBPs that had been the most important factor in preventing international agreement from being reached—a factor cited by the United States in 1955 for discontinuing efforts to deal with RBPs under the auspices of ECOSOC. The adoption of Set, therefore, marks a crucial stage in the evolution of national as well as international approaches to RBPs. It should, moreover, be regarded as a dynamic instrument, capable of being elaborated as the divergences of national points of view are narrowed further.

A number of provisions are addressed to states which, at the national level or through regional cooperation, are called upon to adopt appropriate legislation and implementing judicial and administrative procedures for the control of RBPs, including those of TNCs. Further measures at the international level are aimed at eliminating or effectively dealing with RBPs affecting international trade, particularly that of developing countries. States and regional groupings of states are asked to report annually to the Secretary-General of UNCTAD on steps taken to meet their commitments to the Set. UNCTAD is requested to report annually on developments in RBP legislation and on specific cases of RBPs adversely affecting international trade.

Provision is made for intergovernmental consultations "in regard to an issue concerning control of restrictive business practices" (Section F.4 (a)). UNCTAD is asked to elaborate a model law on RBPs and implement or facilitate technical assistance, and advisory and training programs on RBPs, particularly for developing countries.

Finally, the Set creates institutional machinery, including a review procedure. An intergovernmental group of experts on RBPs is established to provide a forum for consultations. The group is required to undertake various studies and research and make appropriate reports and recommendations on matters within its competence "including the application and implementation" of the Set. The group is, however, precluded from acting as a tribunal or otherwise passing judgment on the activities or conduct of individual governments or enterprises (Section G.4).

Excluded Provisions

In the course of the negotiations the OECD countries successfully resisted the inclusion of certain provisions proposed by the developing and socialist country groups. The developing countries sought to restrict the use of consignments, trademarks and trade name licensing, and "other marketing strategies" which, in their view, had the effect of limiting imports or exports by affiliates located within their borders. Both they and the socialist countries, moreover, sought to circumscribe intra-enterprise agreements. For example, the developing countries considered that the Set should prohibit abusive transfer pricing.

The OECD countries rejected these proposals on the grounds that they were not germane to an antitrust code. Transfer pricing, for example, should, in their view, be regarded as a financial or tax revenue problem rather than as an RBP. They also argued that many of the specific provisions proposed by the other groups could not be implemented because of the vagueness of their wording, and that they would have the effect of discouraging foreign investment.

The question of transfer pricing was, in effect, left to the UN Commission on Transnational Corporations,[45] and negotiations on a UN code of conduct on TNCs soon led to agreement among all participants, including the OECD countries, on the need for a provision designed to curb abusive transfer pricing. The provision so agreed requires TNCs to refrain from applying intra-corporate pricing policies that are not based on relevant market prices, or the arm's length principle, and that accordingly have detrimental economic effects, such as the reduction of the tax base for assessing the entities of TNCs and evasion of exchange-control measures. In addition, problems of transfer pricing have featured prominently in the technical cooperation program of the UN Centre on Transnational Corporations (CTC; see chapter 5).

So far as marketing strategies were concerned, the OECD countries agreed, on the basis of precedents of their own, to condemn the use by dominant firms of licensed or assigned trademarks to prevent the parallel importation of products legitimately bearing the same mark, if the purpose of the practice was to avoid competition. But apart from this, the OECD countries succeeded in avoiding the proscription of parent-affiliate transactions involving marketing strategies.[46]

Finally, the Set contains no provisions on technology licensing, such as had been recommended by the first ad hoc group of experts, though subsequent groups thought that this subject should be left to the UNCTAD negotiations on the transfer of technology. The OECD countries consider that a licenser of confidential technology should be free to set price, quantity, field of use, territorial, and other conditions so long as the licenser does not engage in certain abuses of its rights to the technology. Developing countries, on the other hand, insist on a much broader concept of abusive, and, therefore, illegitimate, restrictions in licensing.

Professor Oesterle suggests that the omission of provisions on technology licensing from the Set does not necessarily mean that licensing restrictions could not be brought within the scope of that document. As he points out, U.S. antitrust laws have been held to justify prosecutions for various abuses of industrial property rights. He quotes an official of the antitrust division of the U.S. Department of Justice (J. Davidow) as stating that, despite the absence of rules dealing expressly with know-how licensing from the Set, the rules laid down by that instrument "are universally applicable to all transactions in goods and services and one would suppose that some or even most know-how transfers involve goods or could be characterized as being a sale of services." Oesterle concludes that the developing countries are "on solid ground" in arguing that the Set regulates abuses of industrial property rights. Indeed, he gives reasons for believing that the language of the Set would support even more severe restrictions on abusive technology licensing than those recognized by U.S. law, especially insofar as such licensing violates the rules against restraints on competition contained in the Set (Subsection D(3)).[47]

The Review Conference of 1985

A review conference was held from November 4–15, 1985, but was unable to reach agreement and requested the General Assembly to decide whether a resumed session of the conference should be convened in 1986.[48] Following consideration of this matter, however, the General Assembly decided to convene a further review conference in 1990.

The main issue that prevented agreement at the review conference, as well as at the fifth session of the intergovernmental group of experts held in October 1986, was the question of effective implementation of the Set. The Group of 77 (G-77) was dissatisfied with the implementation of the Set and considered that developed countries had adopted "an increasingly lenient attitude even to restrictive business practices occurring inside their own countries and applied to international trade transactions." It was suggested that these countries were also using RBPS as a means of circumventing commitments under GATT, and that they had resorted to the imposition of voluntary export restraints on weaker trade partners under agreements which were outside the scope of the Set.[49]

The OECD countries, on the other hand, considered that review of the Set and its implementation was the conference's only legitimate concern. Questions of increased protectionism, including voluntary export restraints, were outside the scope of the conference and needed to be addressed in the forums responsible in this matter. The conference was concerned with the extent to which the Set had been implemented since its adoption in 1980. It was pointed out that the Set was designed to take the form of recommendations, the implementation of which was to be voluntary. In this regard, the governments of OECD countries had continued to develop and apply laws to those RBPS that were the subject of the Set. Several important intergovernmental agreements on the control of RBPS had been adopted and were being implemented. In addition, informal cooperation had continued and expanded both among developed countries and between developed and developing countries.[50] On the question of international institutional machinery, the OECD countries considered that the intergovernmental group of experts had proved to be "a most appropriate and useful forum" and that full advantage had still not been taken of the expert character of the group.

The socialist countries considered that the problem of RBPs was the result of the uncontrolled activity of TNCs, cartels, and other monopolistic organizations, and that the work carried out within the framework of UNCTAD in this field represented an important stage in the restructuring of international economic relations on a just and democratic basis. The question of RBPs was not merely an issue between developing countries and developed market economy countries, since such practices were widely used against socialist countries as well. Responsibility for the effectiveness of the Set lay with the main countries in which TNCs were based.

The G-77 claimed that there had been a deterioration in the area of RBPs since 1980 and cited, as an example, information supplied by the United States to the effect that there had been a profound rethinking in certain aspects of its antitrust policy.[51] This was interpreted by the G-77 as indicating a reduction of the U.S. commitment to competition.[52] The United States, however, denied that this was the case. Certain policies had been reconsidered and vertical restraints were now more frequently found to be acceptable, since they were not, on balance, harmful to competition. Indeed, vertical arrangements, such as those between manufacturers and distributors or between distributors and retailers, often fostered competition in that they made for more vigorous competition among firms at the same horizontal level.

Evaluation

The scope of international action on RBPs envisaged by governments in the 1980s, especially from the industrial countries, is clearly quite different from that which had been contemplated at the Havana Conference in 1947 and the years immediately following. The ad hoc committee on RBPS established by ECOSOC recommended in 1953 the creation of an organization with far-reaching consultative and investigative functions. The draft articles of agreement proposed by the ad hoc committee provided for a procedure whereby any affected member on its own behalf or any member on behalf of any affected person, enterprise, or organization within that member's jurisdiction could present a written complaint to the organization concerning any business practices considered to be restrictive under the definition contained in the relevant article. Such complaints, if considered by the organization to be justified, were to be duly investigated. If, after investigation, the organization decided that the existence of a restrictive business practice had been established, and that this practice affected international trade and was likely to have harmful effects on the expansion of production or trade, the organization could decide to request each member concerned to take "every possible remedial action." It could also recommend to the members concerned remedial measures to be carried out in accordance with their respective laws and procedures. Members could be required to report on the remedial action taken, and the organization was to make public the action taken by the members concerned in any particular case. Members could consult with one another either directly or through the organization concerning particular cases of RBPS. Both the investigation and consultative procedures were to be applicable to both private and public commercial enterprises.

The ad hoc committee's recommendations were submitted on an *ad referendum* basis and no government participating in the committee's work was committed to participation in an agency on the lines proposed. Moreover, the ultimate decision of ECOSOC, as noted earlier, was to shelve the ad hoc committee's recommendations. It is, nevertheless, quite clear that the approach of member countries to the problem was much less radical in recent years than in the late 1940s and early 1950s. Indeed, the condition for intergovernmental agreement on the Set was that no international judgment should be made on the activities or conduct of individual governments or enterprises in connection with a specific business transaction. Even in the OECD, which in 1976 officially condemned enterprise participation in cartels and abusive anticompetitive practices, it is doubtful that the home country of any enterprise would be willing to consult about that firm's conduct abroad or would promise to seek to alter that conduct by law, persuasion, or otherwise.[53] The conclusion has been drawn that:

> It seems certain that nations will not, in the foreseeable future, give the UN the power to investigate or adjudge alleged anti-competitive behavior, or to condemn the antitrust policies of a particular nation. Instead, UNCTAD will, as it has in the past, make studies, usually based on the work of consultants or on records obtained in national proceedings. The developing countries hope that such studies will embarrass companies or their governments into action.
>
> Some harmonization of policy can be expected, as more nations gradually adopt and strengthen antitrust laws and accept the principle that even state-owned enterprises are separate from the state. Harmonization, combined with consultation, may lessen conflict sufficiently to allow the precatory norms of cooperation to be followed more frequently. But an effective international antitrust regime is unlikely to precede the development of free trade and evolution of free markets which would provide it with a raison d'être.[54]

The political climate in the 1980s has been unfavorable to the multilateral institutions, not merely in the field of RBPS but generally. Even the Bretton Woods institutions, which had at one time enjoyed high prestige, especially among the industrial countries, have more recently lost ground in the general trend toward more laissez-faire policies and the privatization of public sector responsibilities both nationally and internationally. Moreover, the views of governments as to which business practices are harmful have also undergone profound changes, particularly in some of the countries that had previously played the most active role in seeking international controls.

The fact remains that an international agreement on restrictive business practices does exist and that it contains provisions, including a review procedure, that permit evolution. Even the International Court of Justice has reached a low ebb with the flouting of its authority by important members, but presumably no one would argue that the court should be disbanded or that the effort to strengthen its surveillance should not continue.

2

Permanent Sovereignty over Natural Resources, Wealth, and Economic Activities

As is well known, the majority of the countries that are now members of the United Nations had not yet become independent when the Organization was established. The increase in membership from the original 51 to 159 in 1987 was due almost entirely to the accession to independence of colonial territories in Africa, Asia, and, to a lesser extent, Latin America. While regional economic commissions for Asia and Latin America were established in the late 1940s, the corresponding commission for Africa was not created until 1958, reflecting the slower rate of decolonization in the African continent.

The acquisition of political and legal sovereignty did not, however, lead immediately to economic independence. Indeed, many observers would argue that for many, if not most, developing countries economic independence has still not been realized. Even in Latin America, where most countries had attained political independence in the nineteenth century, theories of economic dependence have been widely discussed by political scientists and economists throughout the postwar period.

It thus became a primary objective of developing countries within the United Nations to achieve international acceptance of the need for translating political and legal sovereignty into economic independence. Only in this way would it be possible to attain one of the main purposes of the United Nations as set out in the first article of the Charter, "respect for the principle of equal rights and self-determination of peoples."

One of the first manifestations of the movement for economic decolonization was the establishment in 1959 of the UN Commission on Permanent Sovereignty over Natural Resources. The resolution of the General Assembly setting up the commission in December 1958 was entitled "Recommendations concerning international respect for the right of peoples and nations to self-determination." The commission was composed of Afghanistan, Chile, Guatemala, the Netherlands, the Philippines, Sweden, the USSR, the United Arab Republic, and the United States, and its mandate was "to conduct a full survey . . . of the right of peoples and nations to permanent sovereignty over their natural wealth and resources . . . due regard [being] paid to the rights and duties of States under international law and to the importance of encouraging international cooperation in the economic development of under-developed countries."[55]

The classical framework for the contractual rights of foreign companies in colonial territories had been the concession. As Samuel Asante has pointed out:

> Under the concession, the transnational corporation made a direct equity investment for the purpose of exploiting a particular natural resource. In many cases, the concession amounted to a virtual assumption of sovereignty by transnational corporations over the host country's natural resources—an example of the old international economic order. It excluded the host government from participating in the ownership, control, and operation of the undertaking. The transnational corporation was given exclusive, extensive, and plenary rights to exploit the particular natural resource and was in effect assured ownership of that resource at the point of extraction.[56]

It has been suggested that concession agreements were not necessarily, in and of themselves, inimical to the interests of the host countries, and that they were not inherently an instrument of colonialism. Cases had been recorded in the past in which a monarch would grant a concession to a group of his subjects for the development of certain natural resources, with mutual benefits to the crown as well as to the developers. It would, in this view, have been quite possible to include provisions in concession agreements safeguarding the rights and interests of the host countries concerned.

In the circumstances of the times, however, a concession agreement was understood as entitling the foreign company to exclusive appropriation of economic benefits subject to relatively modest fiscal levies; exclusive management; complete control of production and development; and exclusive responsibility for marketing, distributing, processing, and all other "downstream" operations.[57] "In short, the traditional concession regime created an enclave status for the transnational corporation fortified by a regime of economic and legal arrangements so formidable and pervasive that it overtly challenged the sovereignty of the host government over its natural resources."[58]

To protect this regime, traditional principles of customary international law embodied a doctrine of state responsibility for injury to aliens and alien property.[59] Host states were enjoined by international law, as understood by Western governments and jurists, to observe an international minimum standard in the treatment of aliens and alien property. Breach of the international minimum standard was considered to justify exercise of the rights of diplomatic protection by the home state of the alien.

Newly independent countries attacked the doctrine of state responsibility as reflecting the interests of the colonial powers, taking insufficient account of the interests of host countries at a time when the latter, being colonies, were in no position to defend their rights. The response of the developing countries to the international minimum standard was to assert the following basic principles, among other things:

1. States have the sovereign right to control the entry of foreign investment or the acquisition of property in their territories and to regulate the activities of foreign companies in their territories.
2. The right to nationalize foreign property is an inherent

attribute of national sovereignty, and the exercise of this fundamental right is not subject to any condition beyond the duty to pay appropriate compensation, having regard to all the circumstances.

3. State contracts or investment agreements freely entered into with foreign companies are to be observed, subject to the sovereign power of the host state to call for renegotiation or revision or even take unilateral action for the modification of such contracts on the basis of changed circumstances or other public interest.

4. While a host state may grant special incentives or concessions to attract foreign investment in accordance with its development objectives, it is not required to accord preferential treatment to foreign companies.

It was inevitable that concepts of foreign ownership and control should change with the accession of the colonies to independence. In December 1962 the General Assembly adopted a resolution on permanent sovereignty over natural resources, rejecting the concept of investor ownership of natural resources.[60] It was the object of this resolution to establish once and for all the right of states to exercise effective control over the development of their economic resources, and, as they saw fit, to nationalize such resources.

The resolution was adopted by a vote of 87 to 2 with 12 abstentions—a decisive majority. The only industrial country to vote against it was France, which was joined by South Africa. The group abstaining consisted of Burma, Cuba, Ghana, and the socialist countries of Eastern Europe. The latter considered that the resolution did not go far enough, Bulgaria objecting that the resolution amounted to a charter of foreign investment.

The United States had opposed the establishment of the Commission on Permanent Sovereignty over Natural Resources on the grounds that the United Nations should not set itself the task of expounding something that was obvious. Once the commission was established, however, the United States participated actively as a member and played a leading role in the General Assembly's consideration of the subject.[61] The U.S. representative stated that his government "wholly supports every country, including our own, enjoying the full benefit of its natural resources" (A/PV. 1193 p. 31).

A key issue for the industrial countries, led by the United States, was whether the General Assembly's decision would merely assert sovereign rights or whether it would also acknowledge sovereign obligations. For these countries the recognition of obligations was of crucial importance.

The commission's draft provided that "appropriate compensation" should be paid for the taking of foreign property "in accordance with the rules in force in the state taking such measures in the exercise of its sovereignty and in accordance with international law." The United States sought to amend this wording in order to provide that "the owner shall be paid appropriate—prompt, adequate and effective—compensation. . . ." Afghanistan proposed that the text should read "the owner shall be paid adequate compensation, when and where appropriate . . . ," while the Soviet Union introduced a draft statement to precede the paragraph on nationalization and compensation, referring to "the inalienable right of peoples and nations to the unobstructed execution of nationalization, expropriation and other essential measures. . . ." In the view of the socialist countries, the fundamental international principle was that of state sovereignty. The basis of any right to compensation was not some rule of international law but the relevant legislation of the state concerned.

Developing countries generally did not voice support of the socialist country view of the matter, while several of them argued that the U.S. amendment was unnecessary: as Madagascar put it, ". . . compensation could not but be adequate." In response to the general sentiment that all amendments should be withdrawn, the United States did withdraw its proposal regarding "prompt, adequate and effective compensation." The U.S. representative contented himself with stating that the U.S. delegation "was confident that the expression 'appropriate compensation' in . . . the draft resolution would be interpreted as meaning, under international law, prompt, adequate and effective compensation."[62]

The General Assembly also had considerable difficulty in reaching agreement on the manner in which the validity of investment agreements should be asserted. However, with a favorable vote of 53 to 22 with 15 abstentions, the Assembly ultimately adopted a text acceptable to the United States, the United Kingdom, and most of the other industrial countries, as well as to most developing countries, stating that "foreign investment agreements freely entered into by, or between, sovereign states shall be observed in good faith." The resolution also recognized that while, in cases of dispute regarding compensation, national jurisdiction should be exhausted, arbitration or international adjudication could be resorted to "upon agreement by sovereign states and other parties concerned"— the latter being a point of importance for the industrial countries.

Other positive elements in the resolution, as seen by the industrial countries, included a provision that foreign capital should be governed by the terms of its import, by national legislation and by international law—prompting Ambassador Adlai E. Stevenson to point out in a letter to the secretary of the American Bar Association that the resolution "incorporates by reference the requirement of international law that foreign capital shall not be subjected to discriminatory treatment."[63] Also of interest to the industrial countries were the provisions that profits on imported capital should be shared "in the proportions freely agreed upon in each case between the investors and the recipient state"; and that nationalization, expropriation, or requisitioning of property "shall be based on grounds or reasons of public utility, security or the national interest which are recognized as overriding purely individual or private interests, both domestic and foreign."

Taking these considerations into account, the legal adviser to the U.S. Department of State concluded that the resolution

expresses the views of the great majority of the nations of the world. Cast in the form of a declaration, which in United Nations usage is meant to give a resolution particular weight, it represents a consensus of the economically developed and less developed countries. The fact that that consensus includes positive recognition of the obligation to pay compensation where property is taken, to observe investment agreements and agreements to arbitrate and to abide by other requirements of international law should contribute to the enlargement of the international investment climate.[64]

Permanent Sovereignty and International Law

At the first UN Conference on Trade and Development (UNCTAD I) held in 1964, the very first resolution of the conference enunciated certain general principles, of which the third was this: "Every country has the sovereign right freely to trade with other countries, and freely to dispose of its natural resources in the interest of the economic development and well-being of its own people."[65] This principle was adopted by a roll-call vote of 94 to 4 with 18 abstentions. The countries voting against and abstaining were principally from the OECD group, although a number of OECD members voted for the third principle.[66]

It is noteworthy that in the fifth committee of the conference, which had been made responsible for drafting the general principles, France submitted an amendment to add the following words to the third general principle: "in accordance with international law."[67] The apparent intention here was to limit the concept of permanent sovereignty in order to require countries to exercise such sovereignty in a manner consistent with customary international law. As noted below in connection with the discussion of the code of conduct on TNCs, there is disagreement between developed and developing countries as to the appropriateness of such a limitation. While most developing countries recognize obligations under customary international law, such obligations do not, in their view, include a body of generally agreed limitations on the right of free disposal of domestic resources.

Even in developed countries it is acknowledged both by the courts and by scholars that there is considerable uncertainty as to the state of international law with respect to foreign property rights and the compensation to be paid if foreign property is nationalized.

In a celebrated case, known as the Sabbatino case,[68] the U.S. Supreme Court, in April 1964, decided that the act-of-state doctrine precluded U.S. courts from examining the legality of a Cuban decree nationalizing a U.S.-owned sugar company. Noting that where treaties were involved, or where there was a general consensus of opinion as to international law, the act-of-state doctrine might not be applied, the Supreme Court went on to say that

> there are few if any issues in international law today on which opinion seems to be so divided as the limitations on a state's power to expropriate the property of aliens. . . . Certain representatives of the newly independent and underdeveloped countries have questioned whether rules of state responsibility toward aliens can bind the nations that have not consented to them. . . .
>
> The disagreement as to relevant international law standards reflects an even more basic divergence between the national interests of capital importing and capital exporting nations and between the social ideologies of those countries that favor state control of a considerable portion of the means of production and those that adhere to the free enterprise system. It is difficult to imagine the courts of this country embarking on adjudication in an area which touches more sensitively the practical and ideological goals of the various members of the community of nations.[69]

Thus the U.S. Supreme Court recognized the existence of differences of opinion between countries as to the status of international law in this field, and used this as a justification for basing itself on the act-of-state doctrine. In the court's opinion, questions resulting from acts of nationalization were political, not legal, in character and should, therefore, be handled as such by the U.S. government.

This decision, supportive of the views of developing countries, was quickly followed by congressional legislation introduced at the request of a committee representative of American business abroad known as the Rule of Law Committee. The latter committee said that it was "deeply disturbed" by the Supreme Court's decision, fearing that it would have adverse effects on overseas investment, especially in the less developed countries.

The new act precluded U.S. courts from declining to give effect to the principles of international law (which were not, however, defined) in cases of nationalization on the grounds of the act-of-state doctrine, that is, the grounds cited by the U.S. Supreme Court. The Sabbatino case was thereupon reopened, the District Court and Court of Appeals found for Sabbatino and against the Banco Nacional de Cuba, and the Supreme Court declined to review the case further.[70]

Despite this reversal of the U.S. Supreme Court's previous decision, the fact remained that the new legislation had not provided an answer to the original finding of the Supreme Court mentioned above, namely that opinions were sharply divided among sovereign states as regards the limitations on a state's power to expropriate the property of aliens, and that there was, therefore, no agreed body of international law in this field on which reliance could be placed. This has been and continues to be a crucial weakness in the efforts of OECD countries in the United Nations to qualify assertions of permanent sovereignty over natural resources and all economic activities by making them subject to international law.

The rights and wrongs of expropriation are, of course, among the most difficult and delicate of all the problems that arise in relations between TNCs and host countries. On the one hand, respect for contractual obligations is an indispensable ingredient of international economic relations and no viable international structure could exist without it. On the other hand, it cannot be assumed that where a country nationalizes without what might seem to be adequate compensation, there is nothing further to be said. Arbitrary confiscation of property cannot be condoned. But if, for example, a company sets its rate of return so high that it insures itself, in effect, against the possibility of expropriation, it may actually tend to bring about the very outcome that it fears most. If that outcome does occur, the company can hardly expect to collect twice on the same transaction. A host country that feels it has been charged an exorbitant price for the inflow of capital, and that profits have been shifted abroad through transfer pricing, is much more likely to take the view that no compensation is required than a country that considers that it has been fairly treated. These things are very hard to pin down in precise terms, but a reasonable inference is that the stability of arrangements made with developing countries regarding private foreign investment is likely to be a simple function of the fairness of such arrangements. The more demanding a company is, and the more it insists on rates of risk-adjusted return in excess of normal market levels, the more likely is it that agreements will sooner or later be repudiated.

Since degrees of "fairness" are not objectively measurable, it is not surprising that countries are divided on the amount of compensation that should be paid to alien owners of nationalized property. In the United States the issue has centered largely on the requirement of "prompt, adequate and effective compensation"—the phrase used by Secretary of State Cordell Hull in 1938 in his notes to the Mexican government claiming compensation for expropriated agrarian lands owned by U.S. nationals.[71] But Professor Oscar Schachter cites numerous authorities for the view that "The argument that the 'prompt adequate and effective' formula is 'traditional' international law finds little support in state practice or authoritative treaties and monographs."[72] In particular, he quotes Judge Charles De Visscher, a past president of the International Court of Justice, as concluding that state practice in cases of nationalization on a broad scale has substantially qualified the right to full and prompt indemnification for the taking of alien property. Judge De Visscher observed that "nationalization hardly ever permits more than partial compensation calculated less by the extent of damage than by the capacity and good will of the nationalizing State."[73] According to Schachter, even American scholars have increasingly challenged the Hull formula; Wolfgang Friedmann going so far as to state that "It is nothing short of absurd to pretend that the protestation of the rule of full, prompt and adequate compensation . . . in all circumstances is representative of contemporary international law."[74]

Such evidence as is available indicates that even where nationalization disputes have been resolved by lump-sum settlements between the nationalizing country and the home state
of the owner or owners, compensation has invariably amounted
to only a small fraction of full value. Moreover, it has taken
many years to reach such settlements—often ten to twenty
years—and no interest has been paid.[75]

It should be noted that doubts about the Hull formula do not
depend entirely on the fact that nationalization has not *in practice* resulted in the Hull standard of compensation. If this were
the case, the question would still arise whether the states
undertaking nationalization were violating customary international law. But Schachter points out that "in the light of the
existing case law of international tribunals (including two recent arbitral awards by eminent judges . . .) one surely cannot
conclude that the prompt, adequate and effective rule would
be applied generally as existing law by an international tribunal."[76]

It is true that clauses similar to the Hull formula have been
used in bilateral investment treaties between home and host
states, but, as Schachter indicates, this does not mean that such
clauses would be obligatory in the absence of the respective
treaties. Indeed "the very negotiation of such contractual commitments as part of the *quid pro quo* shows that they are not
merely declaratory of existing obligations." Moreover, an earlier State Department legal adviser described such clauses as
an "advance" over customary law.[77]

It would appear that the terms "appropriate compensation"
or "just compensation" would come closest to expressing the
generally accepted requirement of international law in cases of
nationalization. The former term was in fact used in the General Assembly's Resolution 1803(XVII) of 1962 as noted above
and was subsequently endorsed by the U.S. Second Circuit
Court of Appeals in a case that came before it in 1981.[78]

Schachter's view of the standing of the Hull formula has been
challenged by M. H. Mendelson, who cited a number of prewar
and postwar cases in which various claimants were awarded
"just compensation," interpreted by the tribunals as meaning

"full value" or "fair market value" or, as interpreted by the U.S. Supreme Court, the full amount of a fair valuation based on the price a willing buyer would pay to a willing seller.[79]

However, as Schachter pointed out in his reply, the fact that "fair market value" had been awarded in certain cases could not establish the existence of an absolute rule applicable in all circumstances. The tribunals cited by Mendelson had been concerned with the particular facts of the cases before them, not with the interpretation of the Hull formula, which had not in fact been invoked in these cases. What these cases showed was that foreign investors may receive fair awards without asserting an absolute and inflexible rule.

Schachter concludes that the interests of investors are not served by carrying on the debate in terms of the Hull formula, with its negative historical and political overtones in many countries.[80]

Permanent Sovereignty and the NIEO

The principle of permanent sovereignty over natural resources was a key element in the New International Economic Order (NIEO) proclaimed by the General Assembly at its sixth special session in 1974. In particular, the General Assembly declared that the new order should be based on respect for "full permanent sovereignty of every State over its natural resources and all economic activities. In order to safeguard these resources, each State is entitled to exercise effective control over them and their exploitation."[81]

Similarly, the Charter of Economic Rights and Duties of States, adopted at the General Assembly's twenty-ninth regular session in 1974, affirmed the right of states to "freely exercise full permanent sovereignty, including possession, use and disposal, over all its wealth, natural resources and economic activities as well as to regulate and exercise authority over foreign investment within its national jurisdiction."[82]

It will be noted that by 1974 the principle of permanent sovereignty was being applied not merely to natural resources, as in the early decisions in this field, but also to "all economic activities" and to "wealth."

As in the case of the UNCTAD third general principle, a number of leading OECD countries did not accept the NIEO or the Charter of Economic Rights and Duties of States. They were particularly critical of the fact that Article 2 of the charter makes no explicit reference to the applicability of international law, to the treatment of foreign investment, and to the payment of compensation for nationalization. The charter recognizes the duty of the nationalizing state to pay appropriate compensation "taking into account its relevant laws and regulations and all circumstances that the State considers pertinent." The wording of the earlier Resolution 1803, on the other hand, was that appropriate compensation was to be paid "in accordance with the rules in force in the State taking such measures in the exercise of its sovereignty *and in accordance with international law*" (emphasis added).

The sponsors of the charter were, therefore, understood by the OECD countries to be going back on the commitment regarding international law contained in Resolution 1803. This was not, however, the only possible interpretation of the wording of the charter. An alternative interpretation would be that what was rejected was not international law but the view that it was a principle of international law that "appropriate compensation" was to be understood as requiring application of the Hull formula—a view questioned by a number of Western as well as Third World lawyers, as noted above. Consequently, an alternative interpretation of the charter is that while it rejects the Hull formula, and while international law is not explicitly mentioned, it does accept the obligation to pay "appropriate compensation" as prescribed by international law. On this interpretation the failure to refer explicitly to international law in this context was a result of the fact that the OECD countries were insisting that the Hull formula was an inseparable part of international law.

In this connection it should be noted that even the Latin American countries that accept the Calvo doctrine are not thereby denying that international law has a role to play in regard to the treatment of foreign companies. The Calvo doctrine is not about the rejection of international law but about the content and scope of state responsibility.[83] The new nations of Africa and Asia likewise do not reject international legal norms but do consider unacceptable the substance of norms fashioned, as they see it, to serve the narrow interests of an international community that had excluded them at the time the norms were evolving. On the other hand, many of them have accepted bilateral investment treaties and the Convention for the Settlement of International Disputes.[84]

This is not the place or context in which to examine the question how far resolutions of UN organs carried by majority vote—such as the Charter of Economic Rights and Duties of States—could be considered effective in achieving their purposes. Even if such resolutions are adopted unanimously they are not legally binding in the sense in which international treaties are binding. In strictly legal terms, a UN decision by simple majority[85] has as much or as little validity as a decision that is unanimous; but the effectiveness of both types of decision depends on the voluntary response of governments: such response may range all the way from ignoring UN decisions, even when unanimous, to implementing them through domestic legislation even when they are adopted only by simple majorities.

The problems raised by nationalization and the consequential need for compensation have diminished sharply in importance since the mid-1970s. At least four factors have probably contributed to this. In the first place, most of the important foreign-owned mineral-extracting companies in developing countries had either already been nationalized by the mid-1970s or had accepted a degree of local participation in ownership sufficient to satisfy the aspirations of the host countries concerned. Secondly, host governments have come to recognize that their development and revenue objectives can often be best secured by means other than nationalization. Thirdly, the bargaining strength of host countries has been seriously weakened by pressures on their balances of payments, resulting particularly from the debt problem, and these countries have, therefore, sought to avoid policies that might have adverse effects on the inflow of capital whether public or private. Finally, TNCS and other foreign investors, particularly in the resource sector, have become more aware of host country objectives and have adapted their policies to those objectives by readiness to reduce their own equity participation while expanding the types of activities that yield fees, royalties, and other forms of nonequity income.

For all these reasons, North-South frictions resulting from conflicts over the principle of permanent sovereignty over natural resources are no longer of major importance, and a modus vivendi has developed that is likely to last for some time. Even the objections to the term and concept of NIEO lost some of their vigor after the United States came close to accepting them, though with certain limitations, in the following statement: "The international economic order is a system of relationships among all nations. The process of change, therefore, must be through an evolving consensus and takes into account the economic systems, the interests and the ideas of all countries. Thus we are talking about a process, or a broad framework for dialogue and progress as much as an 'order'."[86]

A residue of the old conflicts over principle is to be found in the negotiations on a code of conduct on TNCs, as discussed subsequently. These negotiations have been blocked by old controversies that have become to a considerable extent academic. Recent criticism of the United Nations for allegedly promoting the right of expropriation without adequate compensation is, therefore, based on misunderstanding or misinterpretation or both.

It is significant that the International Law Association, at its meeting in Seoul in September 1986, accepted the principle of permanent sovereignty over natural resources, economic activities, and wealth as a principle of international law, in the following terms:

5. Permanent Sovereignty over Natural Resources, Economic Activities and Wealth.
5.1 Permanent sovereignty over natural resources, economic activities and wealth ("Permanent sovereignty"), is a principle of international law.
5.2 Permanent sovereignty which emanates from the prin-

ciple of self-determination is inalienable. A State may, however, accept obligations with regard to the exercise of such sovereignty, by treaty or by contract, freely entered into. This paragraph is without prejudice to economic integration between States.

5.3 Permanent sovereignty implies the national jurisdiction of a State over natural resources, economic activities and wealth without exempting the State from the application of the relevant principles and rules of international law.

5.4 States have a right to regulate, exercise authority, legislate and impose taxes in respect of natural resources enjoyed and economic activities exercised and wealth held in their own territories by foreign interests subject only to any applicable requirements of international law. Except as expressly agreed by treaty or contract or provided by domestic law, no State is required to give preferential treatment to any foreign investment.

5.5 A State may nationalize, expropriate, exercise eminent domain or otherwise transfer property or rights in property within its territory, and subject to its jurisdiction, subject to the principle of international law requiring a public purpose and non-discrimination, and subject to appropriate compensation as required by international law and to any applicable treaty and without prejudice to legal effects flowing from any contractual undertaking.

The Benefits of Ownership

While the right of expropriation with appropriate compensation had been firmly established, it was far less clear in what circumstances taking over ownership, in whole or in part, would ensure control and how far it would assure the receipt of economic benefits to the extent expected or considered desirable. So long as countries needed the assistance of foreign companies for the exploitation of their natural resources, the views and objectives of such companies could not be ignored. The willingness of the companies to commit resources to such projects was bound to depend on whether they were satisfied with the expected return on capital and on the alternative opportunities available to them elsewhere.

Frequently, moreover, governments were not in a position to obtain the information needed for effective regulation or control, or lacked the skilled manpower required for this purpose. There were many ways in which companies could influence their share of the profits realized without the government being made aware of it.

Thus the assertion of permanent sovereignty over natural resources, fundamental as it was in a political and legal sense, did not by any means settle the question of regulation and control of resource development in the developing countries nor the distribution of benefits resulting from such development. Those countries that were not in a position to take over completely from the TNCs were inevitably required to come to terms with them. In other words, a process of negotiation was required, with each side having certain bargaining strengths and weaknesses. Developing countries needed access to capital, technology, and management in degrees that varied with the stage of economic development that each country had attained. Before a TNC was committed to any particular resource project its bargaining strength was at its highest point, since it was free to withhold its entry into the project unless its minimum conditions were satisfied and unless it could look forward confidently to the realization of a satisfactory rate of return on capital. Once the TNC was committed to a project, however, the balance of bargaining strength would shift to some extent, since withdrawal from the project would involve the TNC in substantial costs. If a country felt that the TNC had imposed unduly demanding conditions as the price for entry, it could force a renegotiation of the basic agreement. Thus the stability of agreements on resource development depended on their being perceived by both parties as fair, not only before the investment had been made but afterwards also.

If, in its turn, the host country proceeded to place excessive demands on a company that had committed substantial resources and was, therefore, no longer free to withdraw, the gain might well be short-lived. For example, in the event of a need for additional investment for purposes of expansion or new exploration, the company concerned might well conclude that it could no longer rely on getting reasonable or stable terms while other companies would be deterred by the previous experience of that company. Thus stability of agreements depended on the exercise of restraint by both host countries and TNCS.

3

The Creation of New International Machinery on Transnational Corporations

Important as the assertion of permanent sovereignty over natural resources was in the process of economic decolonization, still broader issues of national and international economic policy were raised by the growing number and strength of TNCs during the 1960s and early 1970s. Moreover, it was not only the developing countries but the developed countries as well that began to perceive possible conflicts between the objectives of nation-states and those of the TNCs. On the one hand, there was a general belief that a company that made a profit on its business transactions made an equivalent contribution to social welfare. This idea was summed up tersely in the famous remark of U.S. Secretary of Defense Charles E. Wilson: "What is good for the country is good for General Motors, and what's good for General Motors is good for the country."

On the other hand, there was also a growing awareness that in certain circumstances this proposition might not be true, and that a calculus of social costs and benefits might differ considerably from private costs and benefits. One example with which people were becoming increasingly familiar was that of industrial pollution. The discharge of industrial waste into the atmosphere or into lakes, rivers, and oceans represents a massive cost to the community, but this cost is not usually charged to the companies that are responsible, so that there is a divergence between profitability to the company and profitability to the community in such a case.

Consequently, there is no general presumption that can be made about the relationship between costs and benefits resulting from private foreign investment.

Apart from these general considerations, there was a perception on the part of many host countries in the 1960s that TNCs frequently created enclave economies within the borders of the host country. This was particularly common, it was thought, in the mining industries that were often established in remote areas of the host countries and which could extract resources from the ground and ship them abroad without transferring much of the benefits to the countries concerned.

In some cases such companies would exert pressure on local governments to minimize their tax obligations or to obtain from them special concessions, not only in the field of taxation but in financing an extensive infrastructure in the form of construction, transport, power, and other facilities required. Cases were even cited in which companies had interfered in local politics with a view to ensuring the installation of governments that would be most likely to be responsive to TNC requirements. From this it was only a short distance to the bribery of local officials in order to obtain favors of one kind or another. It was often suggested by the companies in this context that they were not themselves responsible for initiating bribery and corruption, but that they had to fall in with the ways of the local community if they were to conduct their business at all. While there may have been a certain truth in this in some cases, it was difficult, at best, to disentangle local and foreign responsibility.

These were some of the considerations that prompted governments to examine the possibilities of national and international regulation of TNC behavior.

The Colloquia at Amsterdam and Medellin

Side by side with the growing recognition of the need for regulation of TNC activities, there was a sense that if the resources and capabilities of TNCs could be appropriately directed, they could make a contribution to world development of considerable magnitude and significance. Thus, in the course of the 1960s, the United Nations began to consider the means for promoting private foreign investment in developing countries. Resolutions in this sense were adopted by the General Assembly in 1965, by UNCTAD in 1964 and 1968, and by ECOSOC in 1967.[87]

In August 1968 ECOSOC noted that, despite the importance of the role that foreign private investment, properly integrated into the development programs of developing countries, could play in the economic growth of these countries, efforts to promote such investment at both the national and international levels thus far had not succeeded in achieving the rate of increase that was desirable. The Secretary-General had suggested that it might be helpful to arrange a dialogue between host governments and foreign investors to enable them to define their attitudes on the role and conditions of foreign investment in developing countries, each with a full knowledge and understanding of the other's viewpoint. In accepting this idea, the council pointed out that such a dialogue "would provide useful information on the aims and interests of the parties concerned and might make it possible to establish bases of reconciliation and to formulate new promotion measures to be put before the developing and developed countries."

Accordingly, the council authorized the Secretary-General to convene a panel on foreign investment for the above purposes.[88] The panel duly met at the Amstel Hotel, Amsterdam, February 16–20, 1969.

Invited to participate in the panel on foreign investment were high-ranking officials of governments of developing countries, largely at the ministerial level or governors of central banks, leading executives of manufacturing and financial enterprises in the industrialized countries, and representatives of regional and international agencies concerned with economic development and financial institutions. In selecting members of the panel the Secretary-General took into account the requirements of equitable geographical distribution and the need for numerical limitation, in order to bring about a frank and close exchange of views.

Mr. Philippe de Seynes, Under-Secretary-General for Economic and Social Affairs, was elected chairman. The panel also elected a steering committee composed of Mr. A. Alikhani, minister of economy (Iran); Mr. Sumio Hara, president, Bank of Tokyo (Japan); Mr. Pieter Kuin, Unilever N. V., Rotterdam (Netherlands); Mr. Carlos Massad, governor, Central Bank of Chile (Chile); Mr. Tom J. Mboya, minister for economic planning and development (Kenya); and Mr. David Rockefeller, president, Chase Manhattan Bank, New York (United States of America).

Following its discussions, the meeting was able to adopt an "Agreed Statement."[89] The statement recognized that if private foreign investment were to contribute fully to the development objectives of the developing countries, it must find its place within the framework of the national development program and policies of each host country. The panel considered that this would call for better all-around understanding of the rights and obligations of the host countries, private investors, and governments of the industrialized countries.

It was accepted that governments of host countries were the best judges of their own development objectives and of the means to be employed in achieving these objectives. The diversification of the economies of these countries was creating a wide variety of investment opportunities, and there was a need for making those opportunities more fully known to potential investors. The panel considered that

> ... joint ventures ideally provide a highly desirable arrangement for bringing together foreign private capital, host Governments and local entrepreneurs. Accordingly, the Panel agreed that promotion of partnerships utilizing foreign and domestic capital and enterprise in the form of joint ventures should be encouraged along flexible lines. Attempts should be made to secure participation of local capital (including that from regional sources) either by means of partnerships or by issues or sales of stock to the public. The Panel recognized that the extent of such participation in individual projects would have to depend on

a variety of factors such as public policy, local conditions, availability of domestic capital and entrepreneurship, nature of the project, technology needed and other relevant factors. It was recognized that, for reasons of public policy or lack of adequate resources in the developing countries, a number of projects have to be developed under the sponsorship of Governments or public sector organizations, and foreign investment may be associated in these endeavours and encouraged to play its part.

While recognizing that host governments should give due encouragement to private foreign investors, the panel stressed that enterprises thus established should always behave as "good citizens" of the host countries, and, in particular, should maximize the utilization and development of local physical and human resources.

The panel pointed to national development banks as the institutions best capable of acting as catalysts in attracting foreign investment and of developing capital markets to mobilize domestic private capital. Such banks had the advantage of combining specialized knowledge of finance and industry with a familiarity with local conditions and problems.

The panel noted that there was a considerable variety of financial institutions operating in developing countries, and the basic problem was to coordinate their activities and improve their effectiveness by strengthening their technical and financial resources. Such improvement called for joint action by both investing and host countries.

The panel considered that the transfer of technical and managerial know-how to developing countries through foreign investment was frequently as important as the capital provided, if not more important. Steps were needed to increase the absorptive capacity of developing countries as well as their ability to develop new techniques for their own special needs. This called for an increase in research and development and training activity. There was also a need for wider dissemination of information on the various types of contractual arrangements available for transferring industrial technology, such as the li-

censing of know-how, the licensing of turnkey and management contracts, and the more conventional methods of internal
transfer between affiliated enterprises.

The second panel on foreign private investment was held in
Medellin, Colombia, June 8–11, 1970. Being intended to focus
its attention on issues arising in the Latin American region,
the panel was held under the joint auspices of the United Nations, the Organization of American States, and the Inter-
American Development Bank. The government of Colombia
and the International Association of Industrialists (ANDI) acted
as hosts. The convening of the panel provided an opportunity
for both domestic and foreign investors to meet with officials
of Latin American governments, international agencies, and
Latin American regional organizations. Proceeding on the basis
of the discussions that had taken place in Amsterdam, and of
the agreed statement adopted at that meeting, the second panel
tackled the subject in depth from the point of view of the Latin
American region.

On this occasion no attempt was made to draft an agreed
statement. Attention was concentrated rather on obtaining a
clearer understanding of the points of view of the various interested parties involved in foreign investment activities and
defining the issues arising from them.[90]

The rapporteur's report[91] pointed to the need for close collaboration between governments, local investors, foreign investors, and international agencies, guided by a global rather than
nationalist view of development requirements. It was recognized that Latin America must develop its own resources in a
context of regional cooperation in addition to expanding its
relationships with the dynamic forces of business enterprise in
the advanced areas of the world.

Investments by international corporations had already contributed to Latin American development, and it was felt that
the area would be able to gain from a still higher level of participation by the international business community in the region through direct private investment and other mutually
beneficial activities.

Various evaluations and appraisals had been made of the effects of foreign investment in Latin America and some of these

were presented to the second panel. Some of these studies reached the conclusion that the host countries had obtained net benefits from foreign investment, while others pointed to possible adverse effects on balances of payments, particularly where net remittances abroad had increased during the frequent crises experienced in the Latin American countries.

The point was made that it was up to the host governments to adopt policies that would ensure the maximum possible benefits to the economies of the recipient countries from foreign investment. It was felt that such policies should provide attractive and equitable conditions for foreign investors within the framework of national and regional priorities. It was also necessary for Latin American governments to define development targets and priority areas and to follow stable economic policies having the effect of stimulating productive activities. Objective, constructive, and stable criteria should be negotiated between governments and international corporations in order to promote desirable inflows of investment. The inflow of capital could also be stimulated through regional and subregional cooperation. It was suggested that the adoption of regionwide common policies toward foreign investment would be advantageous.

The second panel also addressed the question of possible conflicts between the global policies of TNCs and the national interests of developing countries. Questions were raised regarding the issues of the external locus of company decisionmaking and of foreign equity control.

While some foreign investors said that equity control was essential to their willingness to invest abroad, others indicated their readiness to accept and even seek local equity participation. Host country representatives argued that the acquisition of control of existing domestic companies by foreign investors could create adverse reactions in both the public and domestic private sectors in Latin America which could have a negative effect on the overall climate for foreign investment.

An additional source of tension was created when laws in the country of origin of the foreign investor were given extraterritorial effect or were in direct conflict with the investment or fiscal policies of the host countries. It was considered that such conflicts should be the subject of government-to-government negotiations such as those provided for in double taxation treaties.

It was recognized that the improvement of the climate for foreign investment in Latin America would be enhanced by sound development policies as well as by a vigorous expansion of the domestic private sector. It was suggested that this requires, on the side of the host governments, policies that do not discriminate between foreign and domestic companies, though it was understood that governments had the right to limit or prohibit foreign participation in certain domestic sectors. On the side of foreign investors, recognition was required of the need for seeking the participation of local management and, when appropriate, domestic capital. It was also necessary for domestic companies to avoid restrictive practices that would be an obstacle to increased efficiency and competitiveness.

Transnational corporations were urged to contribute vigorously to expanding exports of manufactured and semimanufactured products from Latin America to the industrially developed countries. The corporations could also make a major contribution to technological progress in Latin America, though there was a need for adaptation of the technologies developed in the industrial countries to the different factor availabilities and costs of developing countries. At the same time certain problems had to be faced, particularly the pollution of the environment.

The Group of Eminent Persons

Questions concerning the conduct of TNCs were raised in the course of discussion of the world economic situation in ECOSOC in the summer of 1972. The Secretariat's *World Economic Survey 1971* (E/5144, p. 10) had stated that: "While these corporations are frequently effective agents for the transfer of technology as well as capital to developing countries, their role is sometimes viewed with awe since their size and power may surpass the host country's entire economy. The international community has yet to formulate a positive policy and establish effective machinery for dealing with the issues raised by the activities of these corporations." In a statement to the council, the Under-Secretary-General for Economic and Social Affairs, Philippe de Seynes, had pointed out that the very size of many of these corporations made it questionable whether such centers of economic power should operate in an institutional vacuum. The representative of Chile referred to damage caused by political interference in his country's affairs by the International Telephone and Telegraph Corporation (ITT). In view of the serious consequences of such interference, he suggested that the council should study the matter in depth. It should establish a group of high-ranking independent experts to make a comprehensive study of all TNCs, whatever their origin or influence. That study should then be taken up by an intergovernmental group and ultimately by ECOSOC itself, which should make recommendations for action at the national and international levels.

Following an extended discussion of these statements, the council unanimously adopted Resolution 1721(LIII) on July 2, 1972, requesting the Secretary-General to appoint a "group of eminent persons . . . to study the role of multinational corporations and their impact on the process of development, especially that of the developing countries, and also their implications for international relations, to formulate conclusions which may possibly be used by Governments in making their sovereign decisions regarding national policy in this respect, and to submit recommendations for appropriate international action."

In line with the council's decision, the Secretary-General appointed twenty outstanding personalities as members of the Group of Eminent Persons. Those chosen were broadly representative of all the major regions of the world as well as of government, business, academic, and other interests.

The Group unanimously elected L. K. Jha of India as chairman, George Kahama of Tanzania, J. Irwin Miller of the United

States, and Pierre Uri of France as vice-chairmen, and Juan Somavia of Chile as rapporteur.

The Group held three plenary sessions totaling some seven weeks in September and November 1973 and in March–April 1974. An important feature of the work of the Group consisted of hearings that were held during its first two plenary sessions, when it heard testimony and answers to questions from some fifty leading personalities from governments, business, trade unions, special and public interest groups, and universities. This was a novel approach for the United Nations, and proved to be a most useful source of information as well as a valuable occasion for testing ideas. As a basis for the work of the Group, the Secretariat had prepared a comprehensive study entitled *Multinational Corporations in World Development* which set out the facts, analyzed the problems, and discussed various proposals for action.[92]

The Report of the Group

The report of the Group[93] carried the broad support of its members, though the Group was not unanimous on every recommendation in the report—individual members of the Group appended their comments on points of disagreement.

The Group was unanimous, however, in its recommendations for international machinery and action:

At the intergovernmental level we recommend that the Economic and Social Council keep this subject under review on a regular basis. We are convinced that this function can be performed most effectively and most constructively if the Council is supported by a body specifically designed for this purpose. It is for this reason that we attach particular importance to the establishment, under the Economic and Social Council, of a commission on multinational corporations, composed of individuals having a broad and varied experience and a deep knowledge and understanding of the many aspects related to the subject of multinational corporations. As a corollary to this recommendation we recommend the establishment, within the United Nations Secretariat or closely linked with it, of an information and research centre on multinational corporations so that the commission will receive the continuous support it will require to fulfil its mandate.

In its report the Group pointed out that most countries had recognized the potential of multinational corporations[94] and had encouraged the expansion of their activities in one form or another within their national borders.

The role of foreign private investment in development had indeed been acknowledged in the International Development Strategy for the Second United Nations Development Decade.[95] At the same time the Group suggested that certain practices and effects of multinational corporations had given rise to widespread concern and anxiety in many quarters, and a strong feeling had emerged that the current modus vivendi should be reviewed at the international level.

Concerns Regarding TNCs

The Group described the above-mentioned concern and anxieties as follows:

Home countries are concerned about the undesirable effects that foreign investment by multinational corporations may have on domestic employment and the balance of payments, and about the capacity of such corporations to alter the normal play of competition. Host countries are concerned about the ownership and control of key economic sectors by foreign enterprises, the excessive cost to the domestic economy which their operations may entail, the extent to which they may encroach upon political sovereignty and their possible adverse influence on socio-cultural values. Labour interests are concerned about the impact of multinational corporations on employment and workers' welfare and on the bargaining strength of trade unions. Consumer interests are concerned about the appropriateness, quality and price of the goods produced by multinational corporations. The multinational corporations themselves are concerned about the possible nationalization or expropriation of their assets without adequate compensation and about restrictive, unclear and frequently changing government policies.[96]

From all these expressions of concern, the Group said, one conclusion emerged: "Fundamental new problems have arisen as a direct result of the growing internationalization of production as carried out by multinational corporations. We believe that these problems must be tackled without delay, so that tensions are eased and the benefits which can be derived from multinational corporations are fully realized."[97]

The Impact of TNCs on Development

The Group went on to consider the impact of TNCs on development, issues of sovereignty and power, and the distribution of benefits resulting from TNC activities.

With regard to the impact on development, the Group defined the problem as follows:

Multinational corporations have distinct capabilities which can be put to the service of development. Their ability to tap financial, physical and human resources around the world and to combine them in economically feasible and commercially profitable activities, together with their capacity to develop and apply new technology and skills, to translate resources into output and to integrate product and financial markets throughout the world, has proved to be outstanding. Their activities, however, are not *per se* geared to the goals of development. Therefore, the limitations as well as the capabilities of multinational corporations in meeting development objectives need to be clearly understood.[98]

The Group pointed out that while the reduction of inequalities in income and wealth had become a major international preoccupation, TNCs, although they were powerful engines of growth, tended to accentuate rather than reduce inequalities in the absence of proper government policies and, where necessary, social reforms. Moreover, the investments of TNCs did not necessarily or spontaneously flow to the areas where they were most needed for more balanced world development. This was so even in developed countries where private investment tended to concentrate in the relatively more developed regions, so that governments had to make use of public resources in an effort to reduce regional disparities.

The Group drew the conclusion that "it is therefore apparent that private foreign investment is not a substitute for aid."[99] In fact, said the Group, the degree to which developing countries can benefit from private foreign investment is linked with various forms of international economic cooperation, including the volume and terms of official capital flows and trade policies.

A further consideration regarding the impact of TNCs on development was that these companies often concentrated on high technology industries, which did not necessarily serve one of the primary objectives of development, namely, an increase in employment opportunities. Moreover, in countries where TNCs exploited mineral and other resources for export to world markets, the interest of host countries was to secure fair prices for commodities sold and as high a degree of processing as possible within their own borders. The TNCs, guided by their own worldwide marketing strategies, might not pursue the same objective. The Group concluded that, "bearing in mind all these considerations, it is necessary for host developing countries to formulate their development strategies clearly in order to direct the investments of multinational corporations in a way that is consistent with their national goals and policies, including income distribution, labour conditions, industrialization or balance of payments."[100] According to the Group, host countries should specify as precisely as possible the conditions under which TNCs should operate and what they should achieve. They should also indicate the ways in which the activities of TNCs should be integrated into the local economy and fit into the overall priorities of the country.

Issues of Sovereignty and Power

Turning to questions of sovereignty and power, the Group pointed out that "most of the problems connected with multinational corporations stem from their distinctive transnational features in a world that is divided into separate sovereign States."[101]

The Group reported that representatives of both developed and developing countries had indicated that the exercise of direct control over the allocation of one country's resources by residents of another was "a matter of considerable political concern," making the task of harmonizing varying interests and the promotion of the public good by governments especially complex. The size and scope of the larger TNCs made it possible for a few large firms to control substantial shares of local and sometimes world markets. Because of this and their transnational flexibility, they could engage in export market allocation, price discrimination, and transfer pricing, place stringent conditions on the transfer of technology and patents, and enter into cartel agreements that reduce competition. The Group considered that "at present, national and especially international institutions do not deal adequately with the various ways in which multinational corporations can use their power in a manner which may run counter to the needs of the societies in which they operate."[102] It was true, said the Group, that the corporations themselves had a responsibility for regulating their own conduct, and that successful corporate managements usually did so. The Group considered, however, that

... the self-regulatory efforts of multinational corporations should not be over-emphasized. Although multinational corporations are exceedingly effective initiators and organizers of economic activity and growth, they are also reactors to forces and institutions which define the political environment in which they operate. Multinational corporations, then, must be directed towards and constrained from certain types of activity, if they are to serve well the social purposes of development.[103]

Distribution of Benefits

With regard to the distribution of benefits, the Group devoted particular attention to the extent to which host countries, especially developing countries, could develop the capacity to purchase the package of resources provided by TNCs, namely technology, management, capital, and access to markets, at the lowest total cost. The most costly decision a host country could make was to choose the wrong package of resources and much, therefore, depended on the ability to determine which package it would be advantageous to purchase and how best to reshape it so that it could be integrated into the country's total strategy for development. One alternative to the "package deal" was the separate purchase of individual components of the package. The Group noted that some TNCs were ready to accept new forms of operation in which ownership rights were reduced, including management and service contracts, turnkey operations, joint ventures, and coproduction agreements based on national ownership. The Group also saw advantages in providing for agreements of limited duration and for explicit provision for renegotiation.

In addition, developing countries needed to develop their capacity to monitor the pattern of distribution of benefits between themselves and the TNCs operating in their economies. The Group said this issue was "an underlying theme of much of our report."[104] One basic element was involved: host country bargaining ability and power should be increased. The Group believed that "not only should host countries be prepared to use, with fairness and skill, the powers which belong to them as political entities, but they should develop sufficient knowledge to control the impact of multinational corporations on their economies as a whole."[105]

The Group noted that the benefits that developing countries might otherwise derive from foreign investment are often markedly reduced, if not transformed into losses, through intense competition among them in seeking to attract investment by TNCs through the granting of tax concessions and other incentives. It was pointed out that ten-year tax holidays were quite common, as were other arrangements such as exemption from import duties, favorable terms for local borrowing and, above all, the granting of heavy tariff or nontariff protection. In order to avoid the losses resulting from competition among developing countries for the favors of TNCs, as well as to minimize the opportunities for playing off one country against another in securing concessions, the Group recommended that developing countries should undertake cooperative action, notably through the establishment of joint policies in dealing with TNCS.

The Group's Conclusions

Summing up its findings, the Group stated the following:

> Most home countries have the potential to help in steering the activities of multinational corporations into serving the purposes of development. Even with the best of intentions, however, national action may lead to misunderstandings and tensions, unless it is fully explained and discussed. Many host countries, even with the fullest exercise of their sovereignty, may not have the effective means to carry out all the tasks they are called upon to discharge. For all these reasons, we propose the establishment of an appropriate United Nations machinery specifically designed for this purpose, which under the direction of the Economic and Social Council will deal with the issues arising from the activities of multinational corporations and keep the matter under continuous review. The establishment of such an international forum will facilitate discussion, initiate programmes of study and action on various specific aspects, and provide the basis for future institutional developments. Furthermore, a programme of

technical co-operation can assist host, especially developing, countries and the dissemination of pertinent information will benefit all parties concerned.[106]

In amplifying these ideas in the last section of its report, the
Group proposed that a full discussion on the issues related to
TNCs should take place in ECOSOC at least once a year. It recommended further that a commission on TNCs should be established under ECOSOC, and that a center on TNCs should be
set up within the United Nations to improve the flow of information on such issues as restrictive business practices,
transfer pricing, and taxation; to undertake research on the
activities of TNCs; and to provide assistance to governments at
their request with a view to strengthening their capacity to
develop their own policies in this field as well as to negotiate
and implement agreements with foreign investors. In addition,
advisory teams (including economists, engineers, lawyers, and
social scientists) should be made available to governments at
their request to assist them in evaluating investment proposals,
in analyzing proposed contracts and arrangements, and, if desired, to provide technical advisory support to governments in
connection with their negotiations with the TNCs. Finally, the
Group proposed the preparation of a code of conduct on TNCs.

Reservations

As noted above, individual members of the Group of
Eminent Persons did not necessarily subscribe to each and every statement contained in the report. In particular, several of
the members from developed countries, including those from
the Federal Republic of Germany, Sweden, and the United
States, considered that certain of the recommendations had
gone too far in the direction of advocating national and international intervention and regulation. U.S. Senator Jacob Javits,
for example, did not agree with the report in viewing the basic
problem in terms of conflict between the power of TNCs and
the sovereignty of nations, nor with the inference that this
indicated a need to increase the bargaining power of host coun-

tries. Javits stated that this would imply incorrectly that government involvement was preferable to private initiative and that governments know best and would always act in the best interests of their citizens. He and the other members mentioned above felt that there was no necessary conflict of interest between TNCs and host countries and that excessive regulation and control would have the effect of discouraging TNC investment, thereby depriving developing countries of capital and technology that might well be unavailable in adequate amounts except from TNCs.[107] He said that he deplored as strongly as other members of the Group political interference by TNCs in developing countries, but such cases did not represent the typical behavior of TNCs in general. Moreover, a balanced presentation would require acknowledgment of abuses of TNCs by host country governments.

Despite these and other criticisms of the report, Senator Javits, together with all other members in general agreement with his views, stated that he subscribed fully to the major priority recommendation of the report, namely, "to provide a continuing role for the United Nations through a Commission on Multinational Corporations and an Information and Research Centre under Economic and Social Council auspices."[108]

4

Negotiating Standards of Behavior: The Code

The Group of Eminent Persons, referred to in chapter 3 as recommending the establishment of a commission on TNCs, indicated that one of the most important functions of the commission would be to: "Evolve a set of recommendations which, taken together, would represent a code of conduct for governments and multinational corporations to be considered and adopted by the Economic and Social Council, and review in the light of experience the effective application and continuing applicability of such recommendations."

Likewise the General Assembly, in drawing up the Programme of Action on the Establishment of a New International Economic Order at its sixth special session in 1974, urged that "all efforts should be made to formulate, adopt and implement an international code of conduct for transnational corporations":

(a) To prevent interference in the internal affairs of the countries where they operate and their collaboration with racist regimes and colonial administrations;

(b) To regulate their activities in host countries, to eliminate restrictive business practices and to conform to the national development plans and objectives of developing countries, and in this context facilitate, as necessary, the review and revision of previously concluded arrangements;

(c) To bring about assistance, transfer of technology and

management skills to developing countries on equitable and favourable terms;

(d) To regulate the repatriation of the profits accruing from their operations, taking into account the legitimate interests of all parties concerned;

(e) To promote reinvestment of their profits in developing countries.[109]

When the Commission on TNCs was established by ECOSOC in 1974, its program of work expressly mandated it "to secure international arrangements that promote the positive contributions of transnational corporations to national development goals and world economic growth while controlling and eliminating their negative effects."

More recently, under conditions in which the trend—especially in the United States and the United Kingdom—has been deregulation, many observers in the industrial countries see a contradiction in adding to the rules for TNC behavior, especially if the responsibility for drawing up such rules is in the hands of the United Nations.

Yet the antecedents of the idea could not be more respectable. U.S. Senator Jacob Javits was among the earliest to see the usefulness of a UN code of conduct in easing the tensions and conflicts that had arisen between host countries and TNCs. Henry Kissinger, when secretary of state, argued forcefully for such a code in 1975 at the seventh special session of the UN General Assembly, spelling out what it should contain in considerable detail.[110]

Moreover, the OECD adopted a set of "Guidelines for Multinational Enterprises" in 1976. The Guidelines, which take the form of recommendations addressed by OECD member countries to TNCs operating within their territories, lay down standards for the activities of these enterprises. Standards are prescribed in such areas as involvement in local political activities, questionable corporate payments, competition, taxation, employment, industrial relations, science and technology, and disclosure of information. The European Community has also promulgated decisions against restrictive business practices by TNCs operating in the EC.

Within the UN system, several organizations and agencies have been engaged on the formulation of international regulations on specific aspects of the activities of TNCs. UNCTAD's work on RBPs and the transfer of technology has already been mentioned. In 1972 UNCTAD also successfully completed negotiations on a code of conduct in the field of shipping. In 1977 the ILO (International Labor Organization) adopted a tripartite declaration of principles concerning multinational enterprises and social policy. The WHO (World Health Organization) developed a code for enterprises engaged in the production and sale of breast milk substitutes. For a time ECOSOC sought, through an intergovernmental group, to draft an international agreement to prevent and eliminate corrupt practices in international commercial transactions. However, the formulation of the most comprehensive code of conduct relating to the activities of TNCS was entrusted by governments to the Commission on TNCS.

The adoption of a code would, it was argued, be beneficial for both host and home countries. It would establish standards and rules of the game to which host and home countries could look for guidance in matters affecting their relations with TNCs—including the minimum standards of performance considered desirable by the international community as a whole—and would give useful protection to those companies that observe these minimum standards. This is an area in which Gresham's law applies—bad money tends to drive out good. For competitive reasons, it is difficult for a company to maintain the highest standards of performance in matters that involve significant costs if other companies are not being held to certain minimum standards at least. From this point of view a code would assist materially in raising the average level of performance of TNCs. It would also lead to better treatment of TNCs by host countries, not only because of the standards established for such treatment but because any TNC observing the norms of behavior laid down in the code would thereby be entitled to expect and claim corresponding consideration from the host country concerned.

More recently there have been marked changes in the attitudes of both host and home countries to the code. Some of the developing countries, under severe balance-of-payments pressure due to unprecedentedly heavy debt service obligations, have been at pains to reduce the barriers to the entry of private foreign investment. They have, moreover, accepted bilateral investment treaties with home countries that give all the guarantees requested of them regarding fair and nondiscriminatory treatment of TNCS as well as prompt, adequate, and effective compensation in the event of nationalization, without receiving corresponding assurances regarding the behavior of TNCS toward them.

This in turn has led to a growing belief among the home countries that the need for a UN code has been reduced by the network of bilateral investment treaties, and that a multilateral code might actually tend to undermine the bilateral treaties by making them appear one-sided and disadvantageous to the host countries.

The flaw in this approach is that the bilateral agreements may in the longer run prove to be a source of instability in the sense that if a country finds itself in serious difficulties under some provision of such an agreement, it will find a way of avoiding the obligations undertaken, or will request that the clause in question be renegotiated. What TNCS seek above all is stability in their arrangements with the Third World. Such stability is much more likely to be found through the multilateral approach than through the bilateral approach, as has been found in the field of international trade.

Main Issues

One of the most important issues to arise during the early stages of the negotiations was whether the code of conduct should be addressed exclusively to TNCS or whether it should also deal with the treatment of TNCS by governments. The starting position of the G-77 and socialist countries was that the only issue before the working group was the regulation of the conduct of TNCS and that the conduct of governments was outside the purview of the code. The OECD countries, however, made it clear that to stand any chance of acceptance by their governments, the code would have to be a balanced one in the sense of matching the standards of conduct expected of TNCs with corresponding standards to be expected of governments in their treatment of TNCs. Thus the draft code came to include two parts, one dealing with the regulation of the behavior of TNCs and one prescribing standards to be observed by governments in relation to TNCs.

The Legal Nature of the Code

The main issue here was whether the code should be voluntary or legally binding—an issue which had already arisen in the context of the negotiations on RBPS in UNCTAD, as noted in chapter 1.

If the code were to be legally binding on states, it would have to take the form of a multilateral treaty or convention. Provisions of the code affecting the conduct of TNCs would be enforced through national legislation of states adhering to the treaty or convention, or through intergovernmental machinery established for this express purpose.

A voluntary code, on the other hand, would come into operation through a resolution of the UN General Assembly. If such a resolution were adopted unanimously or by an overwhelming majority, it would carry considerable weight, even though it was not strictly mandatory. Such resolutions could ultimately become a source of law both at the national and international levels. For example, individual countries could decide to implement such a code by adopting national legislation, despite the fact that a General Assembly resolution is, in and of itself, not legally binding.

The developing and socialist countries indicated a preference for a legally binding code of conduct, while the OECD countries insisted strongly that any code of conduct would have to be voluntary.

Many lawyers are of the opinion that there is less difference between a voluntary and a legally binding code than might appear at first sight. Negotiations for a legally binding code would undoubtedly need to provide for considerable flexibility in the drafting to make it acceptable to both host and home countries and to assure the cooperation of the TNCs themselves. On the other hand, even if a code were voluntary, few TNCs would feel able to ignore it. As Professor Fatouros has put the point:

> A formally adopted code, even if not in legally binding form, may have important consequences in national and international law . . . ; such consequences may include a "legitimizing" effect (i.e. expressing the world community's approval of particular policies and measures directed at national control of TNCs) and a role as a "source" of domestic and international legal developments, possibly at the behest of domestic groups (e.g. labour unions), particular states or international agencies.[111]

Although the above issue has not been formally settled, all delegations are aware that no code is likely to gain the all-around support that it would need unless it is voluntary. Moreover, the precedent of the code on RBPs, which is voluntary, is a compelling one.

Activities of TNCs

Under the heading "activities," the draft code deals with the standards of behavior to be expected of TNCs, not only in the economic, financial, and social fields, but in the general and political fields as well. A careful examination of the draft code, the text of which is contained in Annex VI, shows that while some issues are still outstanding in this area, there is a large measure of consensus over a substantial body of norms for the behavior of TNCs. Some of these norms reaffirm or restate well-settled principles of international law; others reinforce or define more sharply generally accepted principles of international business practice; while still others break new ground in establishing new standards of corporate conduct. As the Secretariat's fourth survey, published in 1988, points out:

Altogether these provisions may be justifiably characterized as a comprehensive elaboration of the international
concept of "good corporate citizen." Whatever the ultimate
fate of the entire Code of Conduct may be, it is very significant that a global body composed of representatives of
a wide diversity of political and economic systems and
countries at various levels of development, have agreed,
albeit *ad referendum,* on the basic principles of a Code of
Conduct to be observed by TNCs in international business.[112]

In fact it is a widespread view among the negotiators and the
governments they represent that the very process of working
out and securing an intergovernmental consensus on such
norms has had an important influence on TNC conduct even
without the formal adoption of the norms. This is partly because of the indirect participation of business groups in the
negotiations through their close contact with their respective
governments, but partly also because of the direct and active
participation of business groups having the formal status of non-
governmental organizations (NGOs) under the aegis of ECOSOC
and its subordinate bodies: the most active of these has been
the International Chamber of Commerce. Of considerable importance also is the fact that the Commission on TNCs has a
group of expert advisers that meet with the commission and
take part in its deliberations. The expert advisers include representatives of TNCs, and have the right to speak at commission
sessions and to present written documents. By all these various
means there is a continuing dialogue and interaction between
the commission and Secretariat on the one hand and the business community on the other.

The draft code reaffirms well-settled principles based on the
proposition that TNC affiliates are subject to the sovereignty of
the states in which they operate. Some important provisions
of the code on which there is complete agreement among all
groups of countries include:

–TNCs are required to "respect the national sovereignty of
the countries in which they operate" (Annex VI, paragraph
6).
–TNCs must "respect the right of each State to regulate and

monitor accordingly the activities of their entities operating within its territory" (paragraph 8).

—TNCs are expected to "carry on their activities in conformity with the development policies, objectives and priorities set out by the Governments of the countries in which they operate" and cooperate with the host country governments to this end (paragraph 9).

—Contracts between governments and TNCs "should be negotiated and implemented in good faith" and should be subject to review or renegotiation "where there has been a fundamental change of the circumstances on which the contract or agreement was based" (paragraph 11).

—TNCs are required to respect "the social and cultural objectives, values and traditions" (paragraph 12) and "human rights and fundamental freedoms in the countries in which they operate" (paragraph 13).

—A consensus was reached in 1984 regarding the behavior of TNCs in southern Africa, although this has not yet been accommodated in the draft code itself.

There is agreement also on the general principle that TNCs should refrain from interference in the internal political affairs of host states. However, the precise wording is still open to discussion between those who wish the prohibition to be expressed in general terms and those who favor the inclusion of an acknowledgment that some host states permit a limited involvement of TNCs in their internal affairs. Similarly the precise wording of the provision on abstention by TNCs from corrupt practices has yet to be agreed. These are two of many issues outstanding that are not of fundamental importance and that would quickly lend themselves to compromise if the more basic problems of the code could be resolved.

A number of provisions spell out in greater detail the general principle that TNC activities should conform to the broad goals of host states, as noted above. Five wholly agreed paragraphs (21 to 25) relate to ownership and control: two important elements in this context are that TNCs should "make every effort so to allocate their decision-making powers among their entities as to enable them to contribute to the economic and social development of the countries in which they operate" (paragraph 21); and that they should "cooperate with Governments and nationals of the countries in which they operate in the implementation of national objectives for local equity participation and for the effective exercise of control by local partners as determined by equity, contractual terms in non-equity arrangements or the laws of such countries" (paragraph 23).

Other provisions deal with TNC cooperation in support of the balance-of-payments objectives and policies of host countries, avoidance of abusive transfer pricing, compliance with tax laws and regulations, consumer protection, and environmental protection. The code has a paragraph incorporating the relevant provisions of the General Assembly decision on RBPS discussed in chapter 1 and a similar scheme of incorporation is contemplated with respect to the code on the transfer of technology that is still under negotiation in UNCTAD.

An important section of the code deals with disclosure of information by TNCs—an area in which the Group of Eminent Persons had seen a need for major improvement over existing practices. The basic requirement in the code is that TNCs should disclose to the public clear and comprehensive information on the structure, policies, activities, and operations—both financial and nonfinancial—of the TNC *as a whole.* The nature of the information required is spelled out in some detail.

Most, but not all, of the "other provisions" summarized above are fully agreed, and this is reflected in the absence of square brackets (indicating passages not agreed) in the text set out in Annex VI. Thus, for example, the sections on taxation, consumer and environmental protection, and disclosure of information are entirely settled between the parties to the negotiations, and there are, therefore, no square brackets in these sections.

One area in which major issues remain is the transfer of technology. Negotiations in UNCTAD have shown that a solution to the basic conflict of interests in this field is not yet in sight. On the one hand, developing countries seek to bring about the maximum possible transfer of technology and to limit those features of technology licensing that seem to them to prevent such transfer or impose unreasonably restrictive requirements as a condition for such transfer. On the other hand, the TNCs seek to maximize and prolong the gains from the technologies that they control in order to obtain what they regard as a reasonable return on the costs incurred in developing these technologies.

It should also be noted that even where the parties are fully agreed on particular sections of the text, there is often considerable flexibility in the wording of the requirements laid down. This reflects the conflict, or potential conflict, that faces TNCs in reconciling cooperation with the development policies of host countries and maximizing the earnings on their activities in these countries. Thus the obligation of TNCs to contribute to the realization of host country goals is only to "work seriously towards the making of a positive contribution." And their contributions to consumer and environmental protection are to be made "with due regard to relevant international standards."

Although these are only "best effort" requirements hedged about with qualifications, they do establish the important principle that TNCs are to be guided not only by commercial considerations but by the broad development goals of host countries. While some TNCs might see fit to exploit the loopholes in the code to their own advantage, the assumption underlying the code is that most of them would regard the incurring of reasonable costs in cooperating with host countries as a form of sound investment in their own long-run security and profitability. It is in this sense that the already agreed norms and ground rules of international business embodied in the draft code represent an impressive achievement, regardless of the ultimate fate of the code as a whole.

Treatment of TNCs by Governments

Most of the more difficult issues outstanding in the code are to be found in the sections dealing with the treatment of TNCs by governments (Annex VI, paragraphs 47–58). It is, perhaps, not unnatural that defining the obligations of host country governments should have encountered greater difficulties than prescribing the behavior expected of TNCs which, powerful as they are, are subject to the authority of governments. For developing countries, which had initially seen the code as being addressed solely to TNCs, it was already a major concession to accept the idea that host country governments should recognize certain obligations toward the TNCs. They were not prepared to go so far as to allow governments and TNCs to be placed on an equal footing with one another in terms of mutual obligations. To them it seemed clear that TNCs must accept unconditionally the sovereignty of the countries in which they operate and there could not be, even in principle, any counterpart obligation of governments of equal weight or significance.

For the OECD countries, as noted earlier, it was important that the code should be a balanced one, and that the obligations of TNCs toward governments should be matched by corresponding obligations of governments toward TNCs. Some of the provisions in which TNCs and home country governments were most interested related to points of law connected with nationalization and compensation, as well as with jurisdiction. While the obligations of TNCs were, for reasons explained above, defined in fairly flexible terms, there was a tendency on the part of the OECD countries to seek definitions of host country obligations in relatively precise legal terms, despite the fact that those advocating such precision were equally firm on the point that the code should be a voluntary and not a legally binding instrument.

The chapter of the code dealing with the treatment of TNCs is organized under three broad headings: general treatment of TNCs by home and host countries; nationalization and compensation; and jurisdiction, including conflicts of jurisdiction and dispute settlement.

General Treatment

The section on general treatment begins with a fully agreed paragraph of considerable importance: "States have the right to regulate the entry and establishment of transnational

corporations including determining the role that such corporations may play in economic and social development and prohibiting or limiting the extent of their presence in specific
sectors" (Annex VI, paragraph 47).

This paragraph could equally well have been included in the
previous chapter of the code dealing with activities of TNCs. Its
inclusion instead as a paragraph relevant to the treatment of
TNCs by governments signifies that none of the obligations of
governments toward TNCs override the basic rights of states as
defined above.

National Treatment

Of fundamental importance, from the point of view of
the OECD countries and TNCs, is the principle of national treatment; namely that entities of TNCs should be treated by the
countries in which they operate no less favorably than domestic
enterprises.

While developing countries are prepared to concede the general principle of national treatment, they are concerned that
exceptions should be allowable, not only in the interests of
national security—which is a generally agreed exception in all
countries—but also in cases where nondiscriminatory treatment would be prejudicial to domestic development. If, for example, several large TNCs were to obtain the same degree of
access to local banking facilities as domestic enterprises, they
would be likely to preempt an unacceptably large proportion
of locally available bank finance, especially since the domestic
banks might well prefer to have large foreign corporations as
clients rather than less securely established domestic enterprises. Developing countries, therefore, see a need for a development clause that would constitute an exception to the
general provision for nondiscriminatory treatment, but great
difficulty has been experienced in drafting such a clause in a
way that would achieve the good faith objective without simultaneously undermining the basic principle itself.

Nationalization and Compensation

Here the problem has been the traditional one of drafting generally acceptable provisions that would, on the one hand, recognize the right of member states, in the exercise of their sovereignty, to nationalize property within their borders (including foreign property), and that would, on the other hand, recognize the need for just compensation to be paid under due process of law.

Some of the main points of controversy arising in this field have already been discussed in connection with the history of the principle of permanent sovereignty over natural resources, economic activities, and wealth. It was noted there that in 1986 the International Law Association, in accepting permanent sovereignty as a principle of international law, acknowledged the right of a state to nationalize property within its territory, subject to "appropriate compensation as required by international law." A major question in this context is the meaning to be given to the words "as required by international law": here again the substance of the controversy was reviewed at length in the earlier discussion.

The upshot is that several OECD countries, and particularly the United States, continue to maintain that customary international law requires the application of the Hull formula regarding "prompt adequate and effective compensation," despite the considerations adduced by Professor Schachter and others, as set out in chapter 2. This has become one of two key issues in the code negotiations to which further reference will be made below.

Jurisdiction; Dispute Settlement; Conflicts of Jurisdiction

Although paragraphs 55–58 in Annex VI dealing with the above subjects contain numerous bracketed passages, indicating past disagreements among the negotiators, basic agree-

ment or consensus has, according to the Centre on Transnational Corporations (CTC),[113] been achieved on the following
formulations, which would be reflected in the final text of the
code, if and when adopted:

Jurisdiction

(a) An entity of a TNC is subject to the jurisdiction of
the country in which it operates;
(b) TNCs are subject to the laws, regulations, and established practices of the countries in which they operate.

Dispute Settlement

(a) Disputes between host states and TNCs should be
submitted to competent national authorities;
(b) Subject to the consent of the parties, such disputes
may be referred to other dispute-settlement mechanisms;
(c) It is understood that such other dispute settlement
procedures include arbitration and, furthermore, that the
reference to such procedures may derive from agreement
arising before or after the dispute.

Conflicts of jurisdiction over TNCs have raised particularly
acute difficulties among states, and especially among OECD
countries. For example, numerous cases have arisen in which
home country governments have sought to control the activities of overseas affiliates of TNCs in contravention of laws or
policies of the countries in which the affiliates were located.
This issue has, according to the CTC,[114] now been resolved with
the formulation given below, which represents a noteworthy
success in this field.

Where the exercise of jurisdiction over TNCs and their entities by more than one State may lead to conflicts of jurisdiction, States concerned should endeavour to avoid such
conflicts, in particular by seeking to avoid the exercise of
jurisdiction by one State where jurisdiction more properly
appertains to another State, and should endeavour to adopt
mutually acceptable principles and procedures, bilaterally
and multilaterally, for the settlement of such conflicts on

the basis of respect for the principle of sovereign equality and for their mutual interests.

The Two Key Issues

There are two issues that, by common consent, hold the key to ultimate success in the negotiation of the code. Members of the OECD group, in particular, have frequently maintained that if satisfactory solutions could be found in these two areas, the entire code would fall into place. One of these concerns the applicability of the code to enterprises of socialist countries, while the second involves recognition of the force of international law in relation to matters dealt with in the code.

With regard to the first of these questions, an important concession was made by the socialist countries in the course of negotiations within a limited group at the 1983 session. It is the position of these countries that their enterprises operating abroad should not be regarded as TNCs, because, being state owned, they function on the basis of principles that are entirely different from those applying to profit-making TNCs. All other countries consider that, regardless of such differences, all enterprises operating abroad must be subject to the discipline of the code. In 1983 the spokesman for the socialist countries—the representative of the German Democratic Republic—while making it clear that these countries would not accept the designation of any of their enterprises as TNCs, stated that if all other major issues in the code were satisfactorily resolved, the code would be accepted by them as being applicable to their enterprises operating abroad. This was potentially a major breakthrough, but several OECD countries said that it could not be regarded as such unless certain ambiguities in the wording of the concession were removed.

Subsequently, however, agreement was reached *ad referendum* on this difficult issue. The agreement, which remains contingent on the resolution of all other major outstanding issues in the code, provides that the code applies to all enterprises that operate across national boundaries and in any field of activity, irrespective of whether they are privately owned, state owned, or of mixed ownership. It is irrelevant whether or not such enterprises are classified in any country as a TNC. This agreement *ad referendum* was recorded in the report of the thirteenth session of the commission, held in April 1987, as noted in chapter 5.

The second key issue resulted from the view strongly advanced by a number of OECD countries that acknowledgment should be made in the code of the obligations of countries under international law. These countries maintained that it would be much easier from their standpoint to reach agreement on the clauses relating to nationalization and compensation, dispute settlement, and certain other matters if the code contained a general provision recognizing the applicability of international law. One version of such a provision, acceptable to the United States, was the following: "In all matters relating to the Code, States shall fulfil in good faith their obligations under international law."

Some of the G-77 countries contended that there was no agreement as to what constitutes the accepted body of customary international law, and that they were not prepared to agree to any provision that would imply that customary international law might prevail over domestic law. Other developing countries, while ready to accept the force of customary international law, did not agree that it included generally accepted provisions regarding nationalization, compensation, and related matters, as argued by the OECD group.

The G-77 suggested that there was an inconsistency in the OECD position, since the OECD countries were claiming "national treatment" (that is, nondiscrimination) for the TNCs as well as the privilege of being able to appeal to the alleged provisions of customary international law, while no domestic corporation enjoyed that privilege. A compromise proposal advanced by the chairman—the representative of Mexico—on this point (which was acceptable to the G-77) provided that "the principle of the fulfilment in good faith of international obligations will apply to the Code." This wording was not, however, acceptable to the United States and certain other OECD countries because in their view the phrase "international obligations" had become tainted in the course of the negotiations by the fact, as they saw it, that the G-77—or at any rate certain influential members of the G-77—clearly understood that term to exclude customary international law. They also considered it necessary that the provision should refer specifically to the obligations of states.

Numerous other proposals were considered in the course of the negotiations, including one by France that seemed to have wide support—namely that "In all matters relating to the Code, States shall fulfil in good faith their international obligations." This, of course, was close to the chairman's proposal, but made it explicit that the clause was addressed to states.

Despite the strong views expressed on both sides of this contentious question, it is difficult to believe that a mutually agreeable compromise could not have been found if there had been a strong desire in all quarters to adopt a code. The failure to strike such a compromise appears to reflect the lack of a clear overall political decision on the code rather than the difficulty of the particular issue in itself. It had long been clear that neither the OECD countries nor the G-77 could expect to gain a clear-cut victory on the issue of international law—that the final answer would inevitably involve a measure of ambiguity that would enable each side to give its own interpretation of the text adopted. If either side was unwilling to accept such ambiguity, the negotiations were bound to be futile. As long ago as September 1, 1975 U.S. Secretary of State Henry Kissinger, in replying to a question put to him regarding his address to the General Assembly advocating the adoption of a code, had acknowledged the existence of fundamental differences between the United States and many Latin American countries as to the requirements of international law respecting treatment of foreign investors. "It would not be realistic," said Kissinger, "nor is it necessary to resolve this issue in order to develop a useful balanced basic Code for government enterprise relations." If Kissinger's view had been accepted by the OECD countries during the negotiations on the code in the 1980s, the question of the applicability of international law would have been resolved, thereby clearing the way for the adoption of the code as a whole.

Thus, of the two key issues in the code, one has been settled *ad referendum*, while the other could be settled rather quickly if all the OECD countries were prepared to accept a formula already endorsed by a number of them—namely, an affirmation of the need for states to fulfil their international obligations in good faith, bearing in mind that these countries are themselves firmly of the view that the code should not be a legally binding document.

5

Technical Cooperation, Information, and Research

Technical Cooperation

Among the most important of the activities of the Centre on Transnational Corporations (CTC) have been those in the field of technical cooperation. The advisory services of the CTC were designed to address two broad categories of host government concerns; first, the policy, legal and institutional framework relating to foreign investment and technology, and other forms of participation of TNCs in various sectors of the economies of host countries, and secondly, business arrangements in respect of specific projects involving the participation of TNCS.

Advisory services in these two fields did not begin with the establishment of CTC, but had been requested by various governments in earlier years from the technical cooperation services of the United Nations. Such services had been provided particularly in the field of mining. The effect of the establishment of CTC, however, was to enhance UN capabilities along these lines as well as to provide a new source of funding in the form of voluntary contributions by donor governments. These contributions were made to a CTC trust fund for the financing of projects exclusively in the field of relations with TNCS.[115]

In addition to advisory services, CTC has provided training facilities, including workshops and seminars of various kinds.

Particularly important, especially in the early years of CTC, were training workshops for officials of developing countries responsible for the regulation of or negotiations with TNCs. Workshops were designed to strengthen the capacity of officials, primarily from governments but in many cases from the private sector as well, to negotiate effectively with TNCs.

The establishment of a unit within CTC concentrating on problems arising from relations with TNCs meant the building up of a body of experience and expertise specialized in this particular area. In principle, the projects serviced by this unit could have been financed entirely out of UNDP (UN Development Programme) resources. UNDP, was, after all, the central funding agency for UN technical cooperation programs, and governments were increasingly channeling their contributions to such programs through the UNDP. By this means they placed upon recipient governments the responsibility for setting priorities for various domestic claims on multilateral funds for technical assistance. Any government that set a sufficiently high priority on TNC-related projects could always allocate the appropriate proportion of funds made available to it by UNDP.

The principle of central funding was no doubt sound in a long-run perspective. It had, however, always been recognized in the UNDP that small and relatively young agencies such as CTC were invariably at a disadvantage in obtaining access to central funds, because the latter tended to be preempted by well-established and traditional programs that had been planned over a period of years, at times even beyond the UNDP five-year funding cycles. This kind of difficulty was, of course, greatly increased at times of financial constraint, such as prevailed in the mid-1970s, when there was even less leeway than usual for accommodating new activities. The UNDP accepted the fact that under such conditions there was a case for departing from the general principle of central funding.

It was to be expected, of course, that as the CTC program expanded and became better known, and as governments became increasingly aware of the usefulness of the assistance provided under CTC auspices, a gradually increasing proportion of total CTC outlays for technical assistance would be provided by UNDP. This was, in fact, what happened. In recent years UNDP funding accounted for between 55 and 70 percent of total expenditures.

Although the Secretariat had within its ranks a small number of qualified experts with experience of relations between host country governments and TNCS, it was obvious from the beginning that the Secretariat would have to draw extensively on experts recruited for short missions from the outside. Requests for advisory services, particularly, tended to be highly specific, since they usually involved the negotiation of contractual arrangements with TNCS operating in certain particular industries.

In general, CTC concentrated on technical cooperation in the legal, economic, and financial fields. It was not directly concerned with technical problems of industry, agriculture, mining, and the like, such problems being the concern of specialized agencies and other units of the United Nations. Where necessary, CTC cooperated with engineers or other technicians selected by FAO (Food and Agriculture Organization), UNIDO (UN Industrial Development Organization), or other agencies, or by CTC itself.

CTC's comparative advantage lay in the design or drafting of legislation and other regulatory measures, and in assessing the costs and benefits of various types of arrangement with TNCS, as well as ensuring a fair share of the benefits for host countries. Building on its accumulated experience, CTC was able to satisfy the desire of host countries for information on the ways in which other countries had solved such problems for themselves. Very often governments would be faced with TNC proposals for particular sectors of the economy that they were unable to evaluate because of lack of experience in such sectors. They might also be unfamiliar with going rates of royalty, taxation, and other elements having a decisive impact on the distribution of benefits between TNCS and host countries. In such cases CTC was able to be of considerable assistance by interpreting the experience of other countries and helping governments faced with unfamiliar problems to draw their own conclusions as to the course of action they might take.

The home countries and the TNCS were, of course, well aware of the advisory and training roles of CTC along these lines and raised no objection to them. Many TNCs considered that even from their own point of view it would in the long run be preferable to deal with a government that entered into a relationship with its eyes open, understanding the full implications of what it was doing. Attempts to gain excessive advantages from governments that had not been made aware of the full implications of what was being proposed to them frequently proved to be counterproductive: once such governments had gained the necessary experience, and had become aware of any unduly disadvantageous features of agreements into which they had entered, they would generally insist on a renegotiation of terms in order to change the conditions on which the original investment had been undertaken. Stability of agreements between TNCs and host countries was much more likely if the latter entered into such agreements with full knowledge of the way in which the benefits were likely to be shared between the parties concerned.

The CTC has also been able to assist member countries in dealing with cases in which certain TNCs were believed by the governments to be employing abusive transfer pricing methods with a view to reducing the taxable income declared by them in a particular country, or evading the country's exchange controls. Negotiations on the draft code of conduct have led to agreement among all groups of countries that there is a need for provisions that require TNCs to refrain from applying pricing policies that are not based on relevant market prices or the arm's length principle.[116] The problems that arise in practice do not, however, always lend themselves to resolution on the basis of arm's length pricing, since in the nature of the case the setting of intracorporate prices often involves products that are unique to the particular TNC concerned and for which there is no arm's length market. In such cases special methods of investigation and analysis may be needed to determine whether or not abusive transfer pricing has taken place, and if so to what extent.

Where assistance in negotiations is required CTC often engages experts with negotiating experience from leading firms of high reputation in the private sector, practicing in law and

accountancy, or from the investment banks, often on conces-
sional terms. This makes it possible for low-income developing
countries, many of them with severe foreign exchange problems, to gain access to top-level financial, legal, or technical
expertise. Here again the willingness of private sector firms to
offer services on favorable terms no doubt reflects a belief that
bargains struck at the negotiating table are more likely to prove
stable if they are fair to host countries as well as to TNCs, and
are entered into by host countries with a full understanding of
their financial, legal, and technical implications.

One point on which home countries and TNCs took strong
positions for some years was that CTC officials or experts should
not themselves negotiate on behalf of governments in dealing
with TNCs. This issue was discussed at length at the third session of the commission held in April/May 1977, and the points
made were repeated periodically at subsequent sessions of the
commission. The report of the third session reflected the general tenor of these points as follows:

> A number of delegations expressed concern about the pos-
> sible involvement of the Centre in direct negotiations.
> Those delegations urged that the Centre give primary at-
> tention to building up the negotiating capacity of develop-
> ing countries, particularly the least developed nations, but
> that it refrain from involving itself in the actual negotia-
> tion of specific agreements. They suggested that many de-
> veloping nations already had substantial negotiating skills,
> as was evidenced by the availability of experts from de-
> veloping nations themselves, and urged that substantial
> attention be paid to the establishment of indigenous in-
> stitutions and negotiating capacities. An adviser funded by
> the Centre could be called on for advice on specific ne-
> gotiations but should not play a direct part in negotiations
> unless funded by one of the parties involved. Some dele-
> gations felt that that principle, which clearly reflected the
> provision in the United Nations Charter about neutrality
> of United Nations staff, needed to be clearly established
> to maintain the integrity of the Centre as an impersonal

source of advice which could contribute towards improving understanding of transnational corporations.[117]

In reply, the Executive Director, Mr. Klaus Sahlgren, stated that CTC had not been involved in actual negotiations, and that its assistance had been limited to staff work. The assistance provided by CTC fell squarely within the pattern of assistance established by the UN system.[118]

There was actually nothing in the rules of UN technical cooperation as laid down by the General Assembly and the Governing Council of UNDP to prevent UN experts or officials from being included in negotiating teams if governments so wished. Such cases had occurred in the past as far back as the stewardship of Paul Hoffman and David Owen, who had been chiefs of the UN technical cooperation program in its early days.

In fact, the Charter does not use the word "neutrality" in referring to the Secretariat. What Article 100 of the Charter requires of members of the Secretariat is that they "shall not seek or receive instructions from any government or from any other authority external to the Organization," and that "they shall refrain from any action which might reflect on their position as international officials responsible only to the Organization."

The above requirements relate to the behavior expected of the Secretariat with regard to issues between member states. They do not appear designed to enforce "neutrality" on the Secretariat with respect to issues arising between member states and private corporations. Still less do they imply that expert advisers funded by CTC should be subject to the rules of "neutrality." The Charter requirement is a complex one, and is implicit rather than explicit. Implicitly, the Charter requires that in assisting member states in their dealings with private corporations, members of the Secretariat should "refrain from any action which might reflect on their position as international officials responsible only to the Organization." Of course, it is open to anyone to argue that any participation whatsoever by members of the Secretariat or UN-employed expert advisers in negotiations on behalf of governments on business matters would, in and of itself, reflect on their position and integrity as international officials, regardless of whether they behaved in an independent and objective manner, free from outside influence. But this would require a rather extreme interpretation of the Charter.

So long as the independence, integrity, and objectivity of advisers, and of the advice rendered, is maintained there is no reason why governments should not be given assistance in negotiations with TNCS.

The role of CTC and of the experts funded by it is, of course, an advisory one: they do not make decisions on behalf of governments, and governments would not wish them to do so. They offer advice and make recommendations. They may join a government team, normally working, like other team members, under the leadership of a senior government official.[119]

It may be noted further that the Secretary-General is empowered under General Assembly Resolutions 1256 (XIII), 1385 (XIV), and 1530 (XV) to provide governments, at their request, with "the services of well-qualified persons to perform duties of an executive or operational character as may be defined by the requesting Governments. . . ." The Secretary-General is authorized further to "negotiate agreements defining the relationship to be established between the United Nations, the experts and the Governments concerned, including the terms and conditions of employment of the experts."

The General Assembly clearly envisaged considerable flexibility in the purposes for which such experts might be employed, especially since their duties were to be defined by the requesting governments. Cases could arise, especially in the least developed countries, in which there was a real need for services of representation in certain highly technical areas in which such countries might be entirely lacking in seasoned negotiators. In a memorandum written in June 1973 the UN Legal Counsel took the position that the above-mentioned resolutions of the General Assembly seemed broad enough to cover the activities of a lawyer successively representing a series of governments in various negotiations. While the Legal Counsel had not been asked to address himself, in the context of this memorandum, to experts other than lawyers, the logic on which he was relying clearly implied applicability to a broad range of expertise.

Program of Work of the Commission and Centre on Transnational Corporations

At its second session in March 1976 the Commission on Transnational Corporations decided that the objectives of the program of work should be the following:[120]

(a) To further understanding of the nature and the political, legal, economic and social effects of the activities of transnational corporations in home countries and host countries, and in international relations, particularly between developed and developing countries;
(b) To secure effective international arrangements for the operation of transnational corporations designed to promote their contribution to national developmental goals and world economic growth while controlling and eliminating their negative effects;
(c) To strengthen the negotiating capacity of host countries, in particular the developing countries, in their dealings with transnational corporations.

The commission decided further that work should be focused on the following five areas:

(a) Work for the purpose of formulating a code of conduct;
(b) Establishment of a comprehensive information system;
(c) Research on the political, economic and social effects of the operations and practices of transnational corporations;
(d) Organization and coordination, at the request of Governments, of technical cooperation programmes concerning transnational corporations;

(e) Work leading to a definition of transnational corporations.

The commission stated that among its various tasks, the formulation of a code of conduct should be assigned the highest priority.[121] The commission pointed out, however, that the various tasks were interrelated and that information, research, and the definition of the term "transnational corporations" needed to be carried forward as quickly as possible in support of work on the code of conduct. It also stressed the great importance that it attached to the program of technical cooperation aimed at strengthening the negotiating capacity of the developing countries: it considered that this work should proceed "concurrently with the work on the code."[122]

The difficulties encountered by the commission in laying down priorities are clearly reflected in the above statements. That there was a need for setting priorities was abundantly clear: the commission had been informed of the fact that not only were other UN organizations and agencies working on various matters relating to TNCs, but there was a very large amount of work going on outside the United Nations which should be taken into account. Given the relatively limited resources of CTC (the permanent professional staff numbering less than thirty) it was essential to ensure that available staff time was devoted to the questions of highest priority.

It proved impossible, however, for the commission to reach complete agreement on the setting of priorities. The report of the second session of the commission contains five annexes reflecting "areas of concern" as set forth by various groups of countries. These annexes are reproduced as annexes to the present volume. Annex I was submitted by the G-77, Annex II by five OECD countries, and Annex III by four socialist countries. In addition to subscribing to Annex I, a group of ten Latin American and Caribbean countries submitted a list of "areas of concern" that could be used as a basis for preliminary work on a code of conduct, set out in Annex IV. Finally, Annex V contains General Assembly Resolution 35 (XXX) of December 15, 1975, condemning corrupt practices, including bribery by transnational and other corporations, and requesting the inclusion of this problem in the work of the Commission on Transnational Corporations with a view to making recommendations on the ways and means whereby such corrupt practices might be effectively prevented.

It takes no more than a glance at the contents of these five annexes to see that it was out of the question for the commission and the CTC to attempt to deal with all the concerns that had been put forward. It is equally clear from successive reports of the commission that members were unable to agree on the priorities that should be adopted by the commission itself as well as by CTC, despite universal acceptance of the need for such priorities.

Under these conditions it was a matter for the Executive Director and his staff to try to steer their way through the conflicting objectives of commission members, and to make sufficient response to the main objectives of each group to achieve acceptance by the commission as a whole of the work done.

On the whole, successive Executive Directors succeeded in retaining the confidence of all groups, although at times there were difficulties and even crises with one group or another. Reference will be made subsequently to some of these, notably the sharp disagreement on an innocent-looking question—that of the very definition of the term "transnational corporations."

Information

The Group of Eminent Persons had placed considerable emphasis on the need for provision of adequate information to governments on matters concerning TNCs. The group's report stated that:

> Throughout its work, the Group was struck by the lack of useful, reliable and comparable information on many aspects of this subject. The availability of pertinent information is central to many issues, such as restrictive business practices, transfer pricing and taxation. Making

available the right kind of information could well be a most important first step in assisting developing countries in their dealings with multinational corporations. Broad areas in which information should be gathered, analysed and disseminated to all interested parties should include legislation and policies of home and host countries; geographical and industrial distribution of activities of multinational corporations; transmission of technology and financial flows; organization, structure, ownership and global strategies of multinational corporations; the effects of activities of multinational corporations on national and international development.[123]

At its third session, the commission took note with appreciation of the CTC's report on the establishment of a comprehensive information system (E/C.10/28) as well as a feasibility study on the extent to which various types of information could be made available (E/C.10/27). The commission was informed that CTC had organized the information system into five areas of information (E/C.10/28, paragraph 8), namely:

(a) Information on individual transnational corporations;
(b) Macro (or aggregate) information;
(c) Laws, regulations and policies relating to transnational corporations;
(d) Contracts and agreements between transnational corporations and government agencies and local enterprises;
(e) Bibliographical and documentary information.

The commission stressed the need for selectivity, and accepted the above-mentioned categories of information to be assembled by CTC. The fact remained, however, that neither the commission nor the Group of Eminent Persons had been able to indicate the manner in which selectivity was to be achieved. Particular difficulty was encountered in relation to the very first of the above-mentioned categories—namely the category dealing with information on individual TNCS. The number of TNCS, no matter how defined, runs into tens of thousands, and it would be a monumental task to assemble all the quantitative data relating to each one of them, on a comparable basis, particularly if the objective was to keep the information up-to-date at all times. Even more difficult is the selection, classification, and evaluation of qualitative data, without which the quantitative material—largely of a financial character—would have little meaning. CTC was therefore faced with the difficult problem of determining how far it could or should go in seeking to assemble a comprehensive collection of quantitative and qualitative information about individual TNCs.

For some years CTC devoted a considerable effort to the preparation of what were known as "corporate profiles." These consisted of fairly lengthy studies of individual corporations. They contained not only the usual financial data of the type normally included in annual reports of the companies concerned, but also information on the principal lines of business and on other aspects of particular interest to developing countries, including company policy and experience in such countries. The preparation of the profiles was subcontracted by CTC to outside experts, and it was unavoidable that their content was quite heterogeneous and the level of analysis and exposition uneven. The CTC would send copies of the profiles in draft to the companies concerned and obtain their comments.

It soon became apparent that the corporate profiles were running into serious difficulties. Apart from the high cost of preparing any considerable number of such profiles, questions arose regarding the accuracy of the financial data and even more regarding the quality of the analysis of nonfinancial aspects. Moreover, if the profiles were to be useful, they would have to be continuously updated, involving repeated clearances with the companies concerned. Since financial constraints alone precluded coverage of more than a small proportion even of the larger corporations, the question arose whether the selection of companies covered by profiles at any particular time corresponded to the practical needs of developing countries for access to information on such companies.

In retrospect it is clear that the original concept and design of corporate profiles posed unmanageable problems, especially for a unit as small as CTC and possessing such limited resources. Yet it was difficult for CTC to discard the idea, which in the minds of the commission members had become a symbol of success in overcoming the information problem in relation to TNCs. The problem was that the overwhelming majority of government representatives in the commission had not themselves had experience of involvement in the monitoring or regulation of TNC activities, and were, therefore, not aware at first hand of what was really needed. To many of these representatives, notably from the developing and socialist groups, abandonment of the corporate profiles by CTC might well have been misunderstood as implying a retreat from the original purposes of CTC as envisaged by the Group of Eminent Persons and the commission. Under these conditions, CTC continued the effort of preparing the corporate profiles much longer than would have been desirable if it had felt free to change course on this matter.

It was, therefore, not until the tenth session of the commission in 1984 that the Executive Director finally informed the commission of the need for change. The commission was told that many if not most of the requests for information addressed to CTC by governments could not be dealt with through the collection and storing of information in advance. A study of these requests had clearly indicated that they related predominantly to specific aspects of negotiations or to other dealings with TNCs on which CTC's data bank threw little or no light. It had also been found that most of these requests for information concerned little known small and medium size companies that were far too numerous to be covered in CTC's information system on a routine basis. Moreover, the questions asked by governments in relation to these small and medium size firms were generally not of a character that could readily be answered from pro forma material.

The Executive Director, therefore, decided that the content of the corporate profiles should be greatly reduced in order to give them a more manageable form, concentrating on quantitative material readily assembled from computerized sources. Moreover, the emphasis of the information system was to be shifted in order to increase CTC's capability to respond as quickly as possible to questions, which, in the nature of the case, could not be foreseen. To this end, greater attention would be devoted to studies of particular industries and industrial sectors, with the cooperation of research staff as well as the information unit.

Much less difficulty arose in relation to the four other categories of information specified. The problem there was not so much that of the sheer quantity of material as other considerations. For example, the development of macro-information about TNCs depended on intercompany comparability and was made difficult by the heterogeneity of fiscal years and of other definitions adopted by various TNCs for reporting purposes. So far as contracts and agreements of TNCs were concerned, the problem was how to secure access to them. CTC soon managed to assemble a good collection of mining contracts and agreements, many of which, notably in the petroleum sector, were often made public by the parties to the agreements. It proved to be much more difficult and time-consuming to obtain access to contracts and agreements in the manufacturing sector. The remaining two categories—those relating to laws, regulations, and policies relating to TNCs, and bibliographical and documentary information—posed fewer difficulties than the others, and a number of important publications were issued from time to time in these fields.[124]

Research

CTC's research also fell into five broad categories, namely:

(a) Studies relating to the code of conduct and to other international arrangements and agreements affecting TNCs;

(b) Analysis of general trends in the nature and extent of the operations of TNCs;

(c) Analysis of the political, social, and cultural impact of TNCs;

(d) Examination of measures to strengthen the negotiating capacity of governments in their relations with TNCs;

(e) Studies of the role of TNCs in selected areas and sectors.

As already noted, the commission had given highest priority in its program of work to the formulation of a code of conduct. While it was for governments to reach agreement on the text of a code, CTC's task was to assist the negotiators by identifying issues that needed to be addressed, undertaking research where necessary to clarify these issues, and presenting an objective interpretation of any differences of opinion between member countries that might exist as well as various options for compromise wording. There was also a need for the commission to be kept abreast of developments relevant to the code, such as trends in bilateral agreements between home countries and host countries, and the progress of negotiations on other codes relating to TNCs, including developments in various regional groupings such as those of the European Community and the OECD as well as of developing countries.

Just as information about TNCs may be developed at both the micro and macro levels, so also may research be undertaken at the global level as well as at the level of individual corporations.

Prior to the establishment of CTC as a separate unit of the Secretariat, the UN Department of Economic and Social Affairs had prepared for the Group of Eminent Persons a comprehensive study entitled *Multinational Corporations in World Development*, which set out the main facts relating to the activities of TNCs, analyzed the problems raised thereby, and discussed various proposals for dealing with them.[125] The commission recognized the usefulness of this document and, at its second session, called for a second integrated study of the political, legal, economic, and social effects of the operations and practices of TNCs as a sequel to the above-mentioned study that had been published in 1973. Accordingly CTC published further comprehensive studies along the above lines in 1978, 1983, and 1988.[126] These studies, in effect, brought together and synthesized most of the research carried out by CTC within the covers of each single volume.

The surveys of 1978 and 1983 indicated a basic continuity in the evolution of TNC activities during the 1970s and early 1980s as well as in TNC relationships with home and host countries. The 1983 survey showed that the foreign activities of the largest TNCs had increased in relation to domestic operations during the period from 1971 to 1980. For these companies as a group the ratio of sales by foreign affiliates to total sales rose from about 30 percent in 1971 to about 40 percent in 1980. Thus the activities of the TNCs had become more transnational, a trend that was broad based across industries and countries. This reflected the growing crosscurrents of investment among industrialized countries and the growing globalization of production, whereby production units were located in areas that were most advantageous from the standpoint of the overall costs and benefits for the corporations involved.

Both surveys noted a growing diversification in the origins and destinations of foreign direct investment flows. There had been a slowing down of the rate of expansion of TNCs based in the United States, the United Kingdom, and France, while others—notably those based in Canada, the Federal Republic of Germany, and Japan—had accelerated their growth abroad. Companies in some of the larger developing countries had also begun to extend their operations abroad, though the amounts involved were still relatively small.

Both surveys noted a continuing concentration of TNC activities in the developed market economies. Over 95 percent of recorded direct investment flows originated in the OECD area and about three-quarters of these flows were channeled to other OECD countries. Within this area, however, a notable change occurred during the 1970s. The U.S. share of the outflow dropped to less than a half, compensated especially by higher shares accounted for by outflows from Canada, the Federal Republic of Germany, and Japan. At the same time the United States share in inflows increased to about one-third, making this country the largest recipient as well as the largest source of foreign direct investment. Among the developing countries, a mere six (Argentina, Brazil, Hong Kong, Malaysia, Mexico, and Singapore) consistently accounted for between one-half and three-quarters of the total inflows into these countries in the late 1970s. The majority of developing countries—especially the low-income countries—had not attracted substantial amounts of private capital and technology flows, and had benefited little from the massive expansion of private bank lending during the 1970s.

TNCs in South Africa and Namibia

Although, as noted above, the CTC has the responsibility for studies of TNCs in all their aspects, including political aspects, it is only in relation to the activities of TNCs in southern Africa that CTC has been involved in continuing assignments on a political topic, as a result of requests from the commission.

It will be seen from Annex I that there were a number of such requests of a political character among the areas of concern listed by the G-77. Particularly important among these were such matters as direct or indirect interference by TNCs in the internal affairs of host countries; and requests by TNCs to home governments to intercede with the governments of host countries in support of their interests. There is no doubt that CTC would have dealt with such problems as they arose if information along these lines had been brought to its attention. Such matters would have been dealt with, for example, in the integrated studies presented to the commission at five-year intervals or as part of the annual survey of trends placed before the commission at its regular sessions. As far as is known, no such information has become available to CTC since it was established, and it is probably fair to conclude that cases of improper activity by TNCs in the political field have been significantly fewer in number in recent years than they were in the 1960s and early 1970s.

There was at first some disagreement within the commission as to the propriety of including political considerations regarding southern Africa among the concerns of the commission and CTC. The OECD countries pointed out that other UN bodies were dealing with this matter, such as the Centre against Apartheid. It was the view of other groups, however, that CTC's responsibility was to study all activities of TNCs, and that there was no reason to exclude such activities in the context of southern Africa.

The result is that CTC received annual requests from the commission to prepare progress reports on TNC activities in southern Africa as well as reports on particular aspects of these activities. Among the points of particular concern to the commission were the extent to which TNCs were, by their very presence, in effect supporting the system of apartheid in South Africa and the illegal occupation of Namibia.

During the commission's annual discussions of TNC activities in southern Africa, views have been divided as to what the TNCs should be expected to do. All delegations participating in the commission's discussions on southern Africa invariably condemned the policies and practices of the South African government relating to apartheid. But while the African countries and the G-77 as a whole maintained that TNCs should withdraw from South Africa and Namibia, or at least curtail new investment, many of the OECD countries contended that such curtailment or disinvestment would hurt the black workers in South Africa and Namibia more than it would hurt the government of the country.

Resolutions adopted by the commission and by ECOSOC on the activities of TNCs in southern Africa have, therefore, always been adopted by majority vote, with the OECD countries either voting against or abstaining. This reflects the strength of feeling on this particular issue, since in general all delegations have cooperated in trying to avoid voting and have adopted decisions by consensus in almost all cases.

Despite the divisions within the commission on this matter, the resolutions adopted have not been entirely without effect. A number of large TNCs have recently sold their South African affiliates or announced their intention of doing so. More than ninety U.S. based TNCs announced total or partial disinvestment with respect to their ownership of South African affiliates in 1985 and 1986. This represents approximately 20 percent of all U.S. TNCs with assets in South Africa. U.S. firms that have recently announced disinvestment actions include General Motors, IBM, Coca-Cola, Honeywell, Exxon, Warner Communications, Eastman Kodak, Bell and Howell, Stanley Works, and General Electric.[127]

CTC has, however, pointed out that most of the TNCs that are disinvesting are maintaining nonequity ties with South Africa through the sales of exports or the licensing of production. Only a few TNCs are breaking all ties, including refusal to export to South Africa. According to CTC, moreover, "the replacement of foreign direct investment by exports and non-equity relationships is not an effective way of challenging *apartheid,* since the goods previously produced in South Africa by the departing transnational corporations and their technology continue to be available to the South African economy."[128]

CTC has stated further that "the changing role of transnational corporations in South Africa is a direct result of the weak economy and the deteriorating political situation in that country, which have been caused by the refusal of the government to make any meaningful move towards the abolition of *apartheid,* in spite of mounting domestic and international pressures." Implicit here is the conclusion that cases of disinvestment by the TNCs are attributable mainly to their own self-interest, prompted by the weakening economy and political deterioration in southern Africa rather than by any sense of conviction, or recognition of responsibilities in the light of UN resolutions.

It is, nevertheless, possible that once having begun the process of loosening their South African ties, TNCs may be impelled to go further along the lines repeatedly requested of them by the commission. Thus the long-run impact of the commission's work in this field may well be substantially greater than its immediate effect.

Meanwhile, a growing number of governments from both industrial and developing countries have adopted economic sanctions against South Africa, including such measures as the prohibition of air links with South Africa, prohibition of new investment and of imports, prohibition of new bank loans, and prohibition of exports of military and police equipment to South Africa. In addition several governments have acted to counter the possibility that restrictive measures imposed on

TNCs by home countries relating to their activities in South Africa may be used by corporations from other countries to their business advantage. This provides an inducement to TNCs to conform to restrictive measures vis-à-vis South Africa by minimizing any consequential competitive disadvantages.[129]

The Hearings on Southern Africa

In order to dramatize the problems raised by TNC activities in southern Africa, ECOSOC, on the recommendation of the commission, decided to hold public hearings on the matter. The hearings were held at UN headquarters September 16–20, 1985, under the auspices of an eleven-member panel of eminent international personalities appointed by the Secretary-General. The chairperson of the panel was Malcolm Fraser, former prime minister of Australia.

Participants from the following categories were invited to attend the public hearings: representatives of member states; representatives of UN bodies, specialized agencies, and other intergovernmental organizations; representatives of national liberation movements in southern Africa recognized by the Organization of African Unity; TNCs; parliamentarians and other public officials; representatives of nongovernmental organizations and national support groups; individual experts; and representatives of the press. The differing views put forward at the hearings were summed up by the panel in its report as follows:

> The view was presented to us that the industrialization process and the modernizing of the economy by transnational corporations would, in the long run, erode the very system of *apartheid*. Further, it was pointed out that transnational companies provided employment opportunities for black workers, often improved the welfare of their black employees through desegregation and, in many instances, did away with discriminatory practices at the work-place, improved opportunities for the advancement of their black workers and took other similar measures. It was suggested

that any international action taken against transnational corporations in South Africa or Namibia would also have an immediate adverse impact on the black population, particularly that portion employed by transnational corporations. Neighbouring States would also face some economic difficulties.

However, it was pointed out that the same processes of involvement by transnational corporations sustained the *apartheid* system and the occupation of Namibia, directly and indirectly. By providing capital and technology, transnational corporations benefited and strengthened the minority régime and provided it with the resources to enforce apartheid. In addition, transnational banks provided the economy with financial resources, while the taxes paid by all foreign entities to the government assisted it in maintaining the military, police and security forces used to enforce apartheid and the occupation of Namibia. It was also observed that whatever benefits employment with transnational corporations had, it affected less than 5 percent of the black labour force. In any case, the amelioration of employment conditions for black workers did not change the system of *apartheid* as such. Finally, it was pointed out that the neighbouring States had publicly and collectively announced that they were willing to share with black South Africans the burden of eliminating *apartheid*. Calls were made for the international community, including the World Bank, to support projects and activities, such as strengthening transportation links, that would reduce the dependence of those countries on South Africa.[130]

The panel itself went on to analyze the situation, reaching the following conclusion:

> The international community is committed to end *apartheid* and the occupation of Namibia. We share this commitment. We are convinced that this commitment must now be translated into decisive action.
>
> Transnational corporations must be part of this action. While transnational corporations should not intervene in the internal affairs of States, business enterprises, as part

of their social responsibility, cannot be oblivious of universally accepted human rights and general rules of moral and social behaviour. . . .

Governments, especially those of the home countries of transnational corporations, and the chief executive officers of transnational corporations operating in South Africa, also have their share of responsibility. They, too, should take whatever measures are necessary, and be prepared to shoulder their part of the responsibility for bringing about the required fundamental changes.[131]

The panel presented a series of complementary and mutually reinforcing measures as the basis for an international program of action to be implemented immediately and simultaneously. Among the measures recommended were:

–immediate disinvestment by TNCs in the military, police and security sector of South Africa.
–making the voluntary oil embargo mandatory.
–cessation of new investment, including reinvestment.
–cessation of new loans and no renewal or roll-over of existing loans.
–prohibition of imports of gold from South Africa.
–active steps by TNCs remaining in South Africa to hasten the end of *apartheid*, for example by complete desegregation of all work and work-related facilities and application of the principle of equal pay and benefits for equivalent work to all workers.
–implementation of decree No. 1 of the United Nations Council for Namibia and termination of business activities in Namibia by all foreign affiliates unless their parent corporations have entered into appropriate arrangements with the United Nations Council for Namibia.[132]

The panel further recommended that if a TNC does not or cannot comply with the above-mentioned recommendations, international organizations, home country governments, financial institutions, and the public at large should adopt the following measures:

(a) The United Nations should publicize a list of corporations that do not comply;

(b) There should be no public procurement from, and no contracts with, companies that do not comply;

(c) Funds should be withdrawn from, or not placed in, companies that do not comply.

Finally, the panel recommended that in the absence of a "major sign of progress" by January 1, 1987, a program of disinvestment from South Africa should be effected and that the Security Council should adopt a resolution to this effect.[133]

Monitoring the Research Program

Monitoring by the commission of the CTC research program has been undertaken with great attention to both the scope and content of the work done. As noted earlier, views were often divided within the commission as to the studies to be undertaken and the priorities to be set. In the absence of agreement among commission members on these matters, the Secretariat had to do its best to satisfy all requirements within the resources at its disposal.

Individual groups and members would invariably take the floor at the annual meetings of the commission to restate their positions on what research ought to be carried out and what should be dropped, and also on the manner in which the research should be conducted and its content. At times the Secretariat was subjected to strong criticism by one or another group for failing to comply with what that group considered to be a fundamental objective of the research program.

Among the main objectives of OECD countries, for example, was to ensure that the industry studies carried out by CTC were acceptable to the industries concerned and discussed fully with them. This concern regarding the research program was the counterpart of the objective of the same countries in the information field, namely to ensure that corporate data in the information system were consistent with, and wherever possible cleared by, the corporations concerned.

Other groups were equally concerned that the factual material in the information system as well as in the research studies was as accurate as possible. But they were also interested in having the Secretariat comply with the requirement that had been laid down not only by the commission but by ECOSOC and the General Assembly that attention should be drawn to any negative features of TNC activities or behavior. In the nature of the case it could not be expected that the industries concerned would welcome mention of negative features, especially where they felt that evaluations along these lines were based on error or misunderstanding. Thus, there were fears on the part of home countries that particular studies might be too critical of allegedly negative TNC behavior, while in other cases members were apt to criticize particular studies for being too influenced by the views of the corporations concerned.

One industry for which a CTC study was subjected to severe criticism by OECD countries was the pharmaceutical industry. This is an industry that has been the subject of controversy in both host and home countries, leading to parliamentary and other inquiries and reports in such countries as the United States and the United Kingdom, some of them severely critical of the industry.[134] Moreover many governments have found it necessary to establish controls designed to prevent the overpricing of drugs as a means of reducing health costs.

When the first of the CTC reports on the pharmaceutical industry came before the fifth session of the commission in 1979, the study was criticized for factual errors and two delegations stated that their governments could not associate themselves with the study in its existing form. The study was also criticized for "unfounded conclusions" and for not taking sufficiently into account "the need to protect intellectual property, issues related to research and development and the risks that pharmaceutical companies take." Moreover, it was suggested that undue stress had been placed on government intervention as a remedy for the alleged shortcomings of the industry. Several delegations expressed their concern that during the preparation of the document their governments and national industry associations had not been contacted in order to verify the facts. Other delegations considered the study useful as describing the structure of the industry, its largest TNCs, the main issues arising and possible policy options for developing countries. These and some other delegations thought, however, that the report did not sufficiently stress the monopolistic behavior and high profits of some of the TNCs in this industry, the measures that developing countries could adopt to increase production, and the role of trademarks and an international system for registering them.

The first group of countries felt sufficiently strongly about this and other studies by the Secretariat to enter into informal discussions with other groups and with the Secretariat on the possibility of setting up a watchdog committee to supervise CTC's research program and perhaps other areas of its work also. The Executive Director, Klaus Sahlgren, made it clear in the course of these informal discussions that he could not accept a watchdog committee, and was ready to resign if one were established. The idea was not pursued to the stage of presenting a formal proposal to the commission, and it seems unlikely that the commission would have approved such a proposal.

As far as is known, there was no precedent for such a proposal in other UN bodies. At times strong criticisms have been made of documents in the economic and social fields presented to the General Assembly and the Economic and Social Council by the Secretariat. But no suggestion has ever been made for the establishment of controls on Secretariat reports. It has, of course, always been understood that the Secretariat's research and other activities should follow the priorities set by the appropriate legislative bodies, and that the work should be organized in such a way as to comply with budgetary limitations. But within these limits it has been recognized that the Secretary-General should have freedom of action in determining the scope and content of studies and reports.

It is noteworthy that Article 99 of the UN Charter states that: "The Secretary-General may bring to the attention of the Security Council any matter which in his opinion may threaten the maintenance of international peace and security." The inclusion of the words "in his opinion" clearly indicates the wide discretion given to the Secretary-General for reporting his views, even in matters as sensitive as those involving the maintenance of international peace and security. The Secretary-General's prerogative under this article of the Charter has been exercised on a number of occasions, and no challenge has ever been made in that regard. Although the Charter does not explicitly give the Secretary-General the same rights in the economic and social fields, it stands to reason that such a right is implied. Moreover, in Resolution 26 (IV), adopted on March 28, 1947, ECOSOC requested the Secretary-General to draw attention to "any economic situations which should receive special consideration and, in particular, such developments as would, in the opinion of the Secretary-General, justify the calling of a session of the Economic and Employment Commission in accordance with its rules of procedure." The functions of the Economic and Employment Commission were subsequently taken over by ECOSOC itself, but during the early postwar years the commission, an intergovernmental body, was responsible for in-depth study of major world economic trends. It will be noted that, following the precedent of Article 99 of the Charter, the use of the words "in the opinion of the Secretary-General" in the ECOSOC resolution gave wide and indisputable discretion to the Secretary-General in addressing economic situations requiring "special consideration."

In 1984 CTC published a second study of the pharmaceutical industry, concentrating this time upon the activities of the industry in developing countries. The second study did not give rise to the same degree of controversy as the first, either within the industry itself or elsewhere. Care had been taken, once again, to enter into full consultation with representatives of the industry, who were given the study in draft for comment. CTC remained free to accept or reject particular comments and the final text was adjusted to the extent necessary.

The procedure whereby industry representatives were given an opportunity to review drafts and submit comments was adopted for all CTC's industrial studies. Informal meetings were held in each case by CTC, with representation from the industries concerned as well as from CTC's research staff. On the whole these arrangements worked smoothly and CTC was able to take the views of the industrial representatives into account without sacrificing its independence. In some cases, the con-

sultations were extended beyond the industries concerned—
for example, to consumers' groups. By this means CTC was able
to meet the needs of developing countries seeking objective
information on particular industries and companies while
maintaining good relations with the latter.

Research on Socialist Country Enterprises

Particular difficulty arose in the commission regarding
the scope of CTC research on TNCs. The OECD countries considered that CTC's reports should deal with the activities of the
enterprises of socialist countries operating abroad in the same
way as they dealt with similar enterprises in other countries.
At the ninth session of the commission, during the discussion
of the CTC report entitled *Transnational Corporations in World
Development: Third Survey*,[135] certain of these delegations expressed their deep regret that the third survey did not deal with
"the activities of transnational corporations based on States
members of the Council for Mutual Economic Assistance
(CMEA)." They submitted a draft resolution (E/C.10/1983/
L.4)[136] in which CTC was requested, in furtherance of the third
survey, to prepare a study on the activities of state-owned enterprises from both developed market economies and centrally
planned economies conducting international operations, in particular their activities in developing countries.[137]

The socialist countries, on the other hand, took the position
that enterprises from their countries were outside the mandate
of the commission, since they differed from TNCs in their aims,
nature, content, scope, and the implications of their activities.
For that reason the enterprises and trading organizations of
socialist countries should not, they believed, be included
within the scope of work of CTC. CTC research should concentrate on the activities of TNCs from the developed market
economies and the negative effects of those activities on development and international relations.[138]

Delegations from developing countries stated that their position on the matter raised by the OECD countries was a purely

procedural one. On the substance of the question they recalled the statement that had been made on behalf of the G-77 at the eighth session of the commission on the issue of the definition of TNCs. That position, as set out in the report of the eighth session of the commission, was as follows:

> One delegation, speaking on behalf of many, stated that even if the question of definition might be regarded as a problem between two groups of countries, the countries on whose behalf he was speaking would continue to be interested in the type of solution that would be worked out. Even though in advocating a code of conduct for transnational corporations, they had originally envisaged it to be addressed mainly to the negative aspects of the operations of transnational corporations from a certain group of countries, there had since then been several notable developments, including the fact that publicly-owned corporations from different groups of countries now conducted significant operations in many developing countries. Therefore, in that changing context, ownership should not be a determining criterion. The main concern was the manner in which corporations operated.[139]

They also referred to the compromise proposal on definition that had been put forward by the chairman of the special session of the commission in March 1983 and that had been accepted by the G-77. This compromise proposal provided that:

> The term "transnational corporation" as used in this Code means an enterprise, comprising entities in two or more countries, regardless of the legal form and fields of activity of these entities, which operates under a system of decision-making, permitting coherent policies and a common strategy through one or more decision-making centres, in which the entities are so linked, by ownership or otherwise, that one or more of them may be able to exercise a significant influence over the activities of others and, in particular, to share knowledge, resources and responsibilities with the others.[140]

In short, the G-77 had accepted the proposition that all enterprises with transnational activities, whether from socialist countries or market economy countries, should be included within the definition of TNCs.

At the fourteenth meeting of the commission's ninth session, the representative of the German Democratic Republic proposed a motion postponing consideration of the draft resolution put forward by the OECD countries to a further session of the commission. This motion was adopted by a vote of 26 to 10, the majority consisting of developing countries and socialist countries and the minority of OECD countries.

The OECD countries expressed "deep concern and disappointment" at the result of this vote. The question was raised, informally, whether the developing countries had changed their position on the question of definition, as reflected in the statement cited above. If, said a number of OECD countries, the G-77 no longer believed that socialist country enterprises should be included within the definition of TNCs, it would, in their view, be pointless to continue the negotiations on the code of conduct since the OECD countries would never accept such a code if it were limited to companies from the market economies.

Developing countries made it clear in reply in these informal discussions that they were in no way departing from their previous position, and that they had voted for postponement of the discussion for procedural reasons only. By this they meant that the time was not yet ripe for insisting on immediate settlement of the question of definition. In taking this position the developing countries were relying in part on statements made by representatives of the socialist countries at the special session of the commission held in March and May 1983 on the code of conduct to the effect that they would have no objection to inclusion of socialist country enterprises within the scope of application of the code, provided that this formed part of an overall settlement of all questions arising on the code. Consequently, as the G-77 saw the matter, the decision to postpone was a tactical one designed to keep open the possibility of universal agreement on the code in due course.

The OECD countries reintroduced their draft resolution on

this matter at the tenth session of the commission, with the same outcome. The commission adopted a motion to postpone consideration to a further session of the commission by a roll-call vote of 30 to 11.[141]

The Secretariat, on its own initiative, had begun a study of the transnational operations of socialist country enterprises without prejudice to the question whether or not such enterprises should be included within the definition of TNCs. Consideration had, in fact, been given by the Secretariat to the inclusion of an annex in the third survey containing the results of this work to date. Press reports in a number of countries had referred to the fact that such an annex had been prepared, and noted that it had been omitted from the final version of the third survey. Questions were addressed by commission members to the Executive Director at the ninth session regarding these press reports, some of which had alleged that the Secretariat had given in to improper influences. The Executive Director replied that it was quite customary for some of the material produced in the course of research not to be used in the final published version. The Secretariat had made its decision on the merits of the case and not as a result of improper influence.

It is, nevertheless, clear that work had been done on socialist country enterprises, in line with the implicit general mandate whereby the Secretary-General may conduct research in any area which, in his opinion, is a matter of international concern. The socialist countries had indicated that their objection was not to the study of socialist country enterprises by UN bodies in general but only to the inclusion of such enterprises within the mandate of the commission and CTC. For example, they had not raised any objection to such studies when carried out by the Secretariat of the Economic Commission for Europe.

This reasoning raised some difficult questions, especially since the Secretariat is a unified entity under the direction of the Secretary-General, and it is for the Secretary-General alone, as chief administrative officer of the United Nations under Article 97, to decide what work should be undertaken by the Secretariat and in which departments. It should be noted that the Secretariat was established under Article 7 of the Charter as a principal organ of the United Nations along with the General Assembly, the Security Council, the former Trusteeship Council, and the International Court of Justice. It does not seem appropriate for UN bodies to attempt to instruct the Secretary-General as to the manner in which he carries out his responsibilities as chief administrative officer, although it must be admitted that this principle has not always been respected.

The Secretariat was, therefore, placed in a difficult position by the strongly contested views expressed within the commission on the question of definition. On the one hand, the Secretary-General's right to investigate any matter of international concern in any way he saw fit needed to be respected. On the other hand, it could have been counterproductive to press an issue in an area of acute sensitivity, as in this particular case. The difficulty was that whichever way the Secretariat decided the matter, it could not avoid giving offence to one party or another.

At the twelfth session of the commission held in April 1986 the representative of the Federal Republic of Germany, with the support of Canada, Italy, and Japan introduced a draft resolution with the following operative paragraph: *"Decides that, for purposes of the mandate and activities of the United Nations Centre on Transnational Corporations, and in view of the principle of universality, the Centre shall include in its work all enterprises engaged in transnational operations, irrespective of form or nature of ownership and country of origin and regardless of whether such enterprises are referred to in any country as transnational corporations."*[142]

After negotiations among the regional groups the above draft was withdrawn by the sponsors in favor of a draft resolution which was recommended by the commission by consensus for adoption by ECOSOC. The draft read as follows:

The Economic and Social Council,
Recalling its resolution 1913 (LVII) of 5 December 1974, in particular the mandate of the Commission on Transnational Corporations, as well as the terms of reference of the United Nations Centre on Transnational Corporations,
Aware of the growing interdependence of issues and of the

roles of enterprises engaged in transnational operations, regardless of form or nature of ownership and country of origin, but with due regard to the relative weight and influence in the world economy,

Conscious of the relevance of the activities of such enterprises and the importance of minimizing their negative effects while maximizing their positive effects,

Requests the Secretary-General, without prejudice to the negotiations on the Code of Conduct on transnational corporations to study ways and means by which the United Nations Centre on Transnational Corporations can take account of the preambular paragraphs above in preparing research, analyses and information and in pursuing other activities, and to report thereon to the Commission at its thirteenth session.

This decision, which was subsequently adopted by ECOSOC, opened the door to a solution of the problem at issue, whereby relevant activities of socialist country enterprises would be brought within the mandate of the commission and the CTC, without prejudice to the question whether there were fundamental differences between TNCs and enterprises of the socialist countries.

With regard to the definition of the term "transnational corporations," the report of the thirteenth session of the commission, held in April 1987 included the following passage:

One representative recalled that the definition of transnational corporations for the draft code of conduct had been agreed upon *ad referendum.* While not necessarily disagreeing with that statement another representative, speaking also on behalf of many delegations, stressed the fact that all principal outstanding issues in the negotiations of the Code had to be seen in relation to each other.[143]

The first representative mentioned was the spokesman for the developed market economy countries while the second was speaking for the socialist countries.

Thus the inclusion of socialist country enterprises within the scope of application of the code of conduct was, in effect, accepted by all countries, including the socialist countries, provided that all other "principal outstanding issues" within the code were also settled.

The fourth CTC survey, *Transnational Corporations in World Development: Trends and Prospects*, published in 1988, contained a brief section on "Enterprises from socialist countries" which gave some basic facts on equity ventures of these enterprises both in the developed market economies and in the developing countries. It was pointed out, among other things, that "By the mid-1980s, state enterprises in socialist countries had established some 590 branches, subsidiaries and affiliates abroad—a figure that can be compared with an estimated 100,000 foreign affiliates of TNCs from the developed market economies."[144]

6

Promoting Foreign Investment and Other Forms of Cooperation

Recent years have witnessed the development of new attitudes to cooperation between UN members and international business. Such cooperation has taken a variety of forms and can be illustrated by developments in three particular areas. One involves the active promotion of foreign investment by a number of agencies of the UN system, the second the establishment of the UNITAR/UNDP Information Centre for Heavy Crude and Tar Sands, and the third the enlisting of the cooperation of international business in protecting the environment.

Foreign Investment Promotion

These three areas, among others, indicate a new approach to international business in the sense of treating TNCs as potential contributors to world development and a safer and healthier world environment. That is not to say that elements of both these approaches were not to be found in the past. On the contrary, even during the period when concern about TNC activities in host countries was at its height, the UN General Assembly almost invariably pointed to the constructive potential of the TNCs. Nor should it be assumed that the need for regulation in certain areas has been abandoned. What we are speaking of is a change of emphasis more than of substance, but, nevertheless, a change of considerable importance.

Views differ as to how durable this change of emphasis is likely to be. Some would argue that the change is motivated primarily by the economic depression that has afflicted many of the developing countries since the escalation of the debt crisis in 1982, prompting these countries to sweep away as many obstacles to foreign investment as possible. Others, while recognizing the significance of the above consideration, believe that there have been other changes of at least equal importance, including a certain disillusionment with the efficiency of public enterprise and a growing disposition to view the TNCS as having the capacity to bring advanced technology and more efficient management to the solution of development problems. To this extent efforts to enlist the cooperation of the TNCS might well outlast the economic recovery of the debtor countries which, however, does not appear to be in prospect until well into the 1990s.

Both the UN Department of Technical Cooperation for Development (DTCD) and CTC have been engaged for many years in activities that are closely related to foreign investment promotion. These have included advisory services on the structuring of investment legislation, policies, and contractual arrangements with a view to attracting foreign investment; training workshops dealing with such matters as project appraisal, financing plans, and negotiations; and international conferences, seminars, and publication programs to disseminate information and analysis that would be helpful in heightening the capabilities of potential host countries to attract foreign investment. Particularly in the case of CTC, however, direct promotional activities were avoided for many years in recognition of the fact that certain socialist and Third World countries were strongly of the opinion that CTC had no mandate to engage in foreign investment promotion. It is a relatively recent development that opposition to investment promotion in the Commission on Transnational Corporations has tended to subside.

DTCD has been much less affected than CTC by the above consideration. Its investment promotion activities have been increasing rapidly since 1983 in the mining, petroleum, and natural gas sectors with the financial support of UNDP and, increasingly, of the World Bank, often with state enterprises of the host countries sharing project costs. Programs include the preparation of prospectuses, the organization of promotion meetings based on these prospectuses and targeting specific investors, and the undertaking of certain precontractual activities with teams of experts in various fields such as geology, engineering, law, and financial analysis. Future activities may include the mobilization of the financial resources required for investment projects. Activities in support of foreign investment in industry have also been undertaken for many years by the UN Industrial Development Organization (UNIDO).

It would be premature to conclude that these various efforts will succeed in reviving foreign equity participation in developing countries. Undoubtedly there are many developing countries that would welcome a major inflow of private foreign capital and that are prepared to give all the guarantees that foreign enterprise may require. But the same factors that have deterred a resumption of commercial bank lending to the major debtor countries of the Third World are also an obstacle to massive new flows of equity capital—including flows that might be generated by some of the new financial devices such as debt-equity swaps. Many TNCs now see considerable advantages in avoiding equity participation in the Third World. They tend to prefer arrangements that bring in various kinds of service income—for example, through management and service contracts and licensing agreements—without putting significant amounts of capital at risk. Thus it may take a number of years before the more welcoming attitude of developing countries and the greater understanding that foreign investors now have of the standards of behavior expected by host countries come together to enhance the flow of private capital.

The UNITAR/UNDP Information Centre for Heavy Crude and Tar Sands

The UNITAR/UNDP Information Centre for Heavy Crude and Tar Sands was established in October 1981 in response to a recommendation of the First International Conference on Heavy Crude and Tar Sands which had been held in 1979 in Edmonton, Canada, under the sponsorship of the UN Institute for Training and Research (UNITAR).[145] The representatives of governments and national and private oil companies, as well as other organizations involved in the oil industry who attended the conference, recognized that the resources of heavy crude and tar sands already identified exceeded several trillion barrels and that the technology existed or was sufficiently close to realization to ensure that these resources could make a significant contribution to the energy requirements of many countries in the near and medium term. Those attending the conference considered that it would be useful to establish a center to promote the exchange of information on the exploration, production, and refining of heavy crude and tar sands. The center established in response to these views, with the approval of the Secretary-General of the United Nations, is a jointly managed activity of UNITAR and the UN Development Programme (UNDP).

The initial founding members of the center that joined with UNITAR and UNDP in funding the project were the U.S. Department of Energy (DOE), Petroleos de Venezuela, S.A. of Venezuela (PDVSA), and the Alberta Oil Sands Technology and Research Authority of Alberta, Canada (AOSTRA). Membership in the center is open to governments, national and private sector companies, universities, and other interested institutions on payment of a membership fee.

A director, appointed jointly by UNITAR and UNDP is responsible for the day-to-day management of the center. An advisory board composed of sponsoring member companies and organizations, which meets semi-annually, advises the two co-managers from UNITAR and UNDP on the overall operations of the center.

As part of its ongoing work program, the center organized the second, third, and fourth international conferences on heavy crude and tar sands in Caracas, Venezuela, in 1982, in Long Beach, California, in 1985, and in Edmonton, Alberta, in 1988.

The center's continuing activities include the provision of

information, advice, and referrals to interested parties on the processing of heavy crude and tar sands. The information provided includes data on resources in place, availability of technical expertise, and environmental and legal requirements for exploration. The UNDP worldwide network of resident representatives is utilized to the fullest extent possible in disseminating information to governments of developing countries, including a quarterly newsletter, the *Heavy Oiler*, which contains information on the latest developments in the field of heavy crude and tar sands.

There has, of course, been a considerable change in the overall energy situation in the world since the first conference on heavy crude and tar sands in 1979. At that time, oil was selling at around thirty dollars a barrel and many thought that the price might double before 1990. The subsequent downturn in oil prices has had a profound impact on the profitability of alternative energy resources, including heavy crude and tar sands. Despite this fact, the sponsors of the center, both public and private, consider it important that work should continue so that its services will be readily available in the event of renewed shortages of oil. According to the U.S. Geological Survey and other leading authorities, the estimated identified recoverable conventional petroleum resources in the world amount to some 795 billion barrels. On the other hand it is estimated that identified recoverable resources of heavy and extra heavy crude amount to over 400 billion barrels for the world as a whole in oil equivalent, while recoverable natural bitumen totals over 375 billion barrels in oil equivalent, based on current recovery technology. It is clear, therefore, that heavy crude and tar sands may, in the long run, considerably prolong the era of hydrocarbon-based energy.

UNEP Cooperation with Industry to Protect the Ozone Layer

Of particular interest as an example of cooperation between agencies of the United Nations and private industry is the work that is being done to protect the ozone layer by the United Nations Environment Programme (UNEP).[146]

Chlorofluorocarbons (CFCs) are chlorine containing compounds that are commonly used as cooling agents in refrigerators and air conditioners, as propellants in aerosol sprays, as cleaning agents for computer components, and in the manufacture of plastic foams. Scientists' work suggested in 1974 that CFCs were rising to the stratosphere, where their chlorine components were attacking the ozone and breaking it down at a very high rate, much faster than the rate at which ozone would normally break up into molecular and free radical oxygen; and furthermore, that the chlorine components were "locking up" the resulting ozone breakdown products in such a way that they could not readily recombine to form new ozone. Thus, according to this hypothesis, CFCs were depleting the stratospheric ozone layer, increasing the likelihood that ultraviolet sunlight would filter through and cause skin cancer, eye damage, and harm to plant and animal life.

This suggestion set alarm bells ringing around the world. As scientific evidence supporting the theories began trickling in, the Governing Council of UNEP in 1976 directed UNEP to deal with this possible threat to the global environment.

In March 1977 UNEP convened an international conference on the ozone layer in Washington, D.C. The conference was attended by experts designated by governments and by international intergovernmental and nongovernmental organizations and industry. In its final report (UNEP/WG.7/25/Rev.1, Annex III, section 4, paragraphs 2 and 3), the conference recommended the adoption of a twenty-one point world plan of action on the ozone layer and the establishment by UNEP of a committee to make assessments of ozone modification and its impact. UNEP was to exercise a broad coordinating and catalytic role.

Later in 1977, the Governing Council of UNEP, at its fifth session, called on the Executive Director to initiate the activities envisaged by the conference in the field of research and to establish the Coordinating Committee for the Ozone Layer (CCOL). (Decision 84(V) C of the Governing Council of UNEP.) The purpose of CCOL was to provide assistance in coordinating international research on the ozone issue, and in carrying out regular assessments of ozone layer modification and the environmental impact of that modification. In view of the importance of cooperation between industry and UNEP, representatives of industry were invited to participate at the CCOL meetings.

At that stage there was no prima facie case against CFCs. But already some governments were concerned. In 1976 Canada had announced it would order the progressive elimination of CFC-11 and CFC-12 and prohibit their use in nonessential aerosol sprays. Two years later the United States prohibited the use of CFCs as aerosol propellants.

As the worldwide investigation of atmospheric trace gases and of photochemistry of the ozone layer broadened, data were collected from ground stations, balloons, rockets, and satellites carrying instruments and scientists. Certain farsighted industry leaders—in part as a result of work ongoing within the CCOL—began to realize that the growing scientific debate might herald the need for alternative products, and at their urging some of the large chemical companies began research into developing safe substitutes for CFCs.

Between 1977 and 1985 UNEP, working through the CCOL, published nine separate assessments of the severity of the threat to the ozone layer in the light of developing knowledge of atmospheric processes and the trends in the release of chemicals into the atmosphere. As more and more data became available, the CCOL's forecasts moved within a progressively narrowing range, with the result that governments and industry groups that had hitherto voiced some skepticism came to accept the validity of the UNEP approach to the problem.

As understanding progressed through the work of the CCOL, UNEP began to expand its ozone program and embarked on the development of a global legal instrument to provide a framework for controlling the increasingly evident danger of ozone layer depletion. In January 1982, at the request of the Governing Council of UNEP (decision 9/13 B of the ninth meeting of the Governing Council, 26 May 1981), the first session of an ad hoc working group of legal and technical experts for the elaboration of a global framework convention for the protection of the ozone layer was convened in Stockholm at the invitation of the government of Sweden. The session was attended by experts from both developing and developed countries, as well as by representatives from a number of organizations, including industry groups, which participated as observers.

The working group provided a forum for legal and political debate over questions that had until that time remained primarily the province of technical experts. Through its participation in the working group, industry began to address the problem from a global perspective. A sense of urgency was introduced by the following developments.

On the basis of measurements taken in the Antarctic in the spring (September–October) of 1984, and of records compiled from the Antarctic since the 1950s, Dr. J. C. Farman and his colleagues at the British Antarctic Survey published startling findings. Their report, which appeared in *Nature* in 1985, found that the ozone layer over the Antarctic had been declining sharply, with recurrent annual September–October depletion of the layer reaching a cumulative 40 percent since the late 1970s. In effect there was a "hole" in the ozone layer over the Antarctic, a hole as big as the United States, or as deep as Mount Everest is high, and the hole was spreading northwards into the latitude of 40° South.

Industry responded strongly to this new evidence. Industry participation in UNEP efforts increased, with a number of business representatives attending the UNEP-convened conference of plenipotentiaries at Vienna in March 1985. On March 22, 1985, on the basis of the draft prepared by the ad hoc working group of legal and technical experts, the Vienna Convention for the Protection of the Ozone Layer was adopted by the conference and signed by twenty countries and the European Community.

After the Vienna conference, cooperation between UNEP and industry continued to increase. Industry, governments, and UNEP all realized that intensive cooperation and information exchange were indispensable if a global agreement was to be reached within a short period. Several companies and trade organizations contributed valuable information.

In the spring of 1986 UNEP convened a two-part technical

workshop in Rome and Leesburg, Virginia, at which countries and organizations—including representatives of industry—presented more detailed evidence than had ever been compiled previously regarding CFC-caused destruction of stratospheric ozone. It was during these workshops that industry put its largest effort into bringing forward important technical information not only about CFCs but also about other ozone-depleting substances as well.

Among the companies attending the Rome workshop, held in May 1986, were Australian Fluorine Chemicals (ATOCHEM), Du Pont, ICF Inc., Imperial Chemical Industries (ICI), Kali Chemie Ag., Montefluos SpA., and the Rand Corporation. The trade associations represented included the British Aerosol Manufacturers Association (BAMA), the Chemical Manufacturers Association (United States) (CMA), the European Council of Chemical Manufacturers Association (CEFIC), the Federation of European Aerosol Associations (FEA), the Federation of European Polyurethane Rigid Foam Associations (BING), and the International Chamber of Commerce (ICC).

Each company and trade association attending the workshop contributed to the store of knowledge and the understanding of future actions required. The Rand Corporation, for example, presented the results of its working paper on long-term emission profiles for five chemicals suspected of contributing to ozone depletion, and provided the session with useful information on current uses and emissions of these substances. CEFIC brought an important perspective to the workshop by underscoring the need for harmonization of formats for data collection and for careful coordination with governments. CMA provided UNEP with valuable estimates of production, use, trade, and emissions of CFCs by countries and regions. All industry representatives contributed to a detailed discussion of alternative propellants and blowing agents.

The second part of the workshop was held in Leesburg, Virginia, in September 1986. It was attended by observers from Allied Chemicals, the Bruce Company, CMA, CRSS Inc., Dow, Du Pont, and the Rand Corporation, as well as from the media with ABC News, the *Boston Globe,* and *Engineering News.* A number of very important documents on the demand for CFCs and the production and emissions of CFCs were brought to the meeting's attention by several groups, including CMA and Du Pont. Immediately after the workshop some companies announced that in their view it would be prudent to take further precautionary measures to limit the growth of CFCs worldwide.

In part through information contributed by industry representatives and others to the two-part workshop, evidence began to surface regarding the ozone-depleting potential of bromine-containing CFC analogues known as halons.

In concert with the technical workshops, UNEP now embarked on a much more aggressive program of legal-technical negotiating sessions. Key representatives from developed and developing countries and also from the European Community became deeply involved in the negotiations. Industry continued its active participation, but it was for governments to decide what should be done.

In September 1987, after a series of intensive negotiating sessions, UNEP convened a second conference of plenipotentiaries in Montreal, Canada, focusing this time on CFCs. Shortly before the conference the fast-food chain, McDonald's, announced that it was phasing out CFCs in its packaging activities; McDonald's announcement exemplified the concern shown by industry in most parts of the world.

At the Montreal conference industry continued its strong participation in UNEP efforts by sending substantial delegations. Many issues proved to be very controversial, particularly those surrounding the control measures to be taken. After a marathon series of negotiating sessions, the Montreal Protocol on Substances that Deplete the Ozone Layer was finally adopted by the conference on September 16, 1987. Twenty-four countries and the European Community signed the protocol.

The Montreal Protocol, which became effective on January 1, 1989, freezes the production of the controlled CFCs at their 1986 levels and provides for 50 percent reductions in the consumption of CFCs by mid-1999. It allows limited production increases to meet very specific situations. Beginning in 1992 the consumption of halons will be frozen at 1986 levels.

In the years from 1977 to 1985 UNEP had gained increasing experience with the dual legal-technical modes of negotiating.

After the Vienna Convention, UNEP began operating in both modes in parallel: UNEP would convene a meeting of scientific experts, and immediately afterward or even simultaneously, legal experts meeting under UNEP auspices would translate the technical conclusions of the scientists into the proper legal drafting format so that negotiations could proceed expeditiously. The effort snowballed: as more and more data were developed through UNEP efforts, the scientific community—and equally importantly, industry as well—came increasingly to recognize the urgency of the problem; and as scientists' perception of the problem was translated into the language of legal-political negotiation, key government representatives were sensitized to the urgency of the situation and to the need for action. In the course of the process the continuity of the chemical industry's participation greatly facilitated the negotiations.

The Montreal Protocol represents a major achievement in the development of international environmental law. The agreement marks one of the first times that the community of nations, working together with the private sector, has anticipated and taken positive steps to manage a world problem before it could lead to an irreversible crisis. The protocol is expected to result in a significant reduction in damage to human health and the environment from ultraviolet radiation and a variety of skin cancers. The benefits in terms of environmental protection are more difficult to measure, but they accrue to all nations, making the Montreal Protocol an agreement of truly global significance.

Recent observations of ozone levels show that there have been declines in these levels substantially greater than those previously anticipated. This will almost certainly make it necessary for further remedial and preventive action to be taken. If so, the experience gained in developing the Montreal Protocol will be invaluable in taking whatever further steps the situation may require.

Annexes

I

Areas of Concern Regarding the Operations and Activities of Transnational Corporations

Note Submitted to the Second Session of the Commission on Transnational Corporations (1–12 March 1976) by the Group of 77

1. Preferential treatment demanded by transnational corporations (TNCs) in relation to national enterprises.

2. Lack of adjustments by TNCs to the legislation of the host countries in the matters, *inter alia*, of foreign investment and policies concerning credits, exchange, fiscal matters, prices, commercial matters, industrial property, and labour policies.

3. The negative attitudes by TNCs towards the renegotiation of original concessions if such exist and if this should be considered necessary by the Government of the host country.

4. The refusal of TNCs to accept exclusive jurisdiction of domestic law in cases of litigation.

5. Direct or indirect interference in the internal affairs of host countries by TNCs.

6. Requests by TNCs to Governments of the country of origin to intercede with the host Government, with actions of a political or economic nature in support of their private interests.

7. The refusal of TNCs to accept the exclusive jurisdiction of domestic law in the question of compensation for nationalization.

8. Extension by TNCs of laws and regulations of the country of origin to the host country.

9. The activities of TNCs as instruments of foreign policy, including for intelligence purposes, contrary to the interests of the host country.

10. The contribution of TNCs in the maintenance of racist and colonial régimes and support of policies of *apartheid* and foreign occupation.

11. The role of TNCs in the illegal traffic of arms.

12. Obstruction by TNCs of the efforts of the host country to assume its rightful responsibility and exercise effective control over the development and management of its resources, in contravention of the accepted principle of permanent sovereignty of countries over their natural resources.

13. Tendency of TNCs not to conform to the national policies, objectives and priorities for development set forth by the Governments of host countries.

14. Withholding of information of their activities by TNCs, making host countries unable to carry out effective supervision and regulation of those activities.

15. Excessive outflow of financial resources from host countries due to practices of TNCs and failure to generate expected foreign exchange earnings in the host country.

16. Acquisition and control by TNCs of national, locally capitalized enterprises through controlled provision of technology among other means.

17. Superimposition of imported technology without any adaptation to local conditions, creating various types of distortions.

18. Failure by TNCs to promote research and development in host countries.

19. Obstruction or limitation by TNCs of access by host countries to world technology.

20. Imposition of restrictive business practices, *inter alia*, on affiliates in developing countries as a price for technical know-how.

21. Lack of respect of the socio-cultural identity of host countries.

II

Areas of Concern Which Relate to Relations Between Transnational Corporations and Governments

Note Submitted to the Second Session of the Commission on Transnational Corporations (1–12 March 1976) by the Delegations of France, the Federal Republic of Germany, Italy, the United Kingdom of Great Britain and Northern Ireland, and the United States of America

Preamble

1. The following is a selection of areas of concern, which in the opinion of the delegations having prepared this document, deserve particular consideration, although not all of these delegations necessarily share all the concerns mentioned herein. These cover broadly effects on economic and social development of the activities and operations of transnational corporations (TNCs) within the framework set by Governments, including positive and negative impacts.

List of areas of concern

2. Areas of concern of particular importance are set out below. The list is non-exhaustive and may be added to or modified in the light of experience.

(1) The extent to which host country legislation and regulations may discriminate, either in favour of TNCs or against TNCs as compared to domestic enterprises, in the treatment of enterprises on the basis of whether or not such enterprises are under foreign control; the extent to which any such discriminatory treatment affects the activities of TNCs as well as the contributions of TNCs to the development objectives of host countries.

(2) The extent to which expropriation of properties undertaken for public purposes related to internal requirements of the countries concerned are non-

discriminatory in application and are accompanied by prompt, adequate and effective compensation.

(3) The extent to which recourse to international arbitration, including that provided by the International Centre for Settlement of Investment Disputes, or other dispute settlement organizations or procedures play a role in the settlement of disputes arising out of the activities of TNCs.

(4) The effect of the presence or absence of a stable investment climate as a factor affecting the ability of TNCs to contribute effectively to development.

(5) The observance and non-observance of contracts and agreements between TNCs and Governments, the consequential issues which arise in the case of non-observance by either party, and the role which contracts may play in the creation of a stable investment climate.

(6) The role which freedom or restriction of establishment by TNCs in countries may have in assisting or hampering economic and industrial development.

(7) The extent to which domestic laws, regulations and practices on social policies help or hinder development of labour relations activities in TNCs.

(8) The extent to which the social policies practised by TNCs help or hinder development of labour relations activities in countries in which they operate.

(9) The effects of TNC operations and activities on employment possibilities and whether these give rise to benefits, e.g., job creation or non-benefits, e.g., strain on indigenous resources of host countries.

(10) The extent to which the presence or absence of declared points of contact within both TNCs and host Governments have assisted or hindered development of an effective and continuing dialogue between the parties concerned.

(11) The effect of TNC operations and activities on the social and cultural identities of host countries, the positive or negative impacts which these may have on such countries and the extent to which host countries make their expectations known in these respects.

(12) The extent to which existing codes of conduct and guidelines concerned with any aspect of the range of issues relating to the activities of TNCs may already exist, including the study of the materials underlying such codes and guidelines, commentaries thereon and the implementation and/or effects of such codes and guidelines upon TNCs and Governments.

(13) Issues relating to co-operation between host Governments and TNCs to ensure the fullest possible attainment of their respective objectives when TNCs invest in host countries, including the extent to which TNCs and host countries state their needs and objectives in a sufficiently clear manner and how such co-operation may be improved for their mutual benefit.

(14) The need to define more clearly the areas of acceptable and unacceptable political activities on the part of TNCs.

(15) The role played by TNCs and Governments in the transfer of technology to host countries, including the types of technology involved, conditions imposed by TNCs and Governments in connection with such transfers, and the positive and negative effects on technology transfers and the framework within which they are made on host country development objectives and the viability of the investment concerned.

(16) The role played by TNCs in fostering development and growth of related industries in host countries and the positive or negative effects of the activities of TNCs on the existing patterns of indigenous supply and production.

(17) The extent to which TNCs endeavour to participate in or ignore local business and regional organizations of host countries, host country regulation of such participation where these exist, and the consequences of TNC and host country actions in this area.

(18) The extent to which TNCs seek to promote indigenization of their operations and activities in host countries, including appointment of staff at all levels, and the extent to which policies adopted by host Governments help or hinder this process.

(19) The extent to which TNCs may help to improve or make worse the working conditions of employees, including workers' health and safety, and the extent to which host Governments make clear their requirements and/or expectations in these respects.

(20) Identification of those countries which have declared policies on conservation and protection of the environment, and the extent to which these may or may not be observed by TNCs operating therein.

(21) The appropriateness or otherwise of the forms in which TNCs allow for participation in the equity of their operations in host countries, and relevant host country policies and the extent to which these are made known.

(22) The extent to which TNCs take host countries' interests into account in the repatriation of capital, remittance of profits, payments of dividends, royalties and management fees, the extent to which the levels at which these are made are constrained by Governments and the effect this may have on the development process.

(23) The extent to which domestic commercial policies, e.g., in relation to restrictive business practices have been developed by host Governments, whether appropriate machinery has been set up by them within which TNCs and Governments may discuss problems of mutual interest and, if so, the extent to which TNCs and/or Governments use these facilities when it would be appropriate for them to do so.

III

Issues Requiring the Attention of the Commission and the Information and Research Centre on Transnational Corporations

Note Submitted to the Second Session of the Commission on Transnational Corporations (1–12 March 1976) by the People's Republic of Bulgaria, the German Democratic Republic, the Ukrainian Soviet Socialist Republic, and the Union of Soviet Socialist Republics

Supporting the list of areas of concern regarding the activities of transnational corporations (TNCs) contained in Annex I, the aforementioned socialist countries propose the following issues requiring the attention of the Commission and the Information Research Centre:

1. The negative attitude of TNCs towards the freedom of organization of workers, labour conditions and the full exercise of trade union rights.

2. The negative impact of TNCs on economic relations between States, particularly by short-term massive capital movements and price policy, aggravating inflation, the monetary and the raw material situation.

IV

Areas of Concern Which Could Be Used as a Basis for
Preliminary Work for a Code of Conduct to Be
Observed by Transnational Corporations

Paper Submitted to the Second Session of the Commission on Transnational Corporations (1–12 March 1976) by the Delegations of Argentina, Barbados, Brazil, Colombia, Ecuador, Jamaica, Mexico, Peru,
Trinidad and Tobago and Venezuela

A. The transnational corporations shall be subject to the laws and regulations of the host country and, in case of litigation, they should be subject to the exclusive jurisdiction of the courts of the country in which they operate

1. This statement is the reflection of an old Latin American concern
which has its origin in the claim of the transnational corporations to a status,
or to be beneficiaries of a privileged treatment, in the country where they
operate. To validate this claim would signify the provision of a preferential and
discriminatory status in favour of foreign enterprises. It would also presuppose
the establishment of different treatment for nationals and foreigners, which
would be unacceptable. But in the last analysis, the exemption of transnational
corporations from the internal juridical order would bring, as a consequence,
injury to the fundamental basis upon which the sovereignty of the State resides,
which implies full competence over the entire area in which the power of the
State is exercised.

2. This statement expresses the concern that the transnational corporations
should adjust their activities strictly to the legislation of the host country in
matters, *inter alia*, of foreign investment, credit, exchange and fiscal policies,
prices and commerce, industrial property, and labour policies. It is considered
that the transnational corporations should be disposed to facilitate conformity
of their activities (including fields of action and *modus operandi*) by the renegotiation of the original concession, if such exists, and if this should be
considered necessary by the Government of the host country. Also, it is im-

portant that the transnational corporations comply with the requests for information that may be made by the Government of the host country.

3. A natural consequence of the subjection of foreign enterprises to national legislation is the existence of an exclusive competence on the part of the courts of the host country to hear any case or litigation that arises from the application of this legislation. On occasion, the foreign enterprise presumes to escape the jurisdiction of the host States by means of private agreements in which it is stipulated that any controversy that may arise concerning the activities of the enterprise shall be resolved by the courts of the country of origin or of a third State, or that they will be submitted to international arbitration. These types of agreements are not acceptable and, in more than one case, are considered nullified of all right by the national laws.

B. The transnational corporations shall abstain from all interference in the internal affairs of the States where they operate

4. At present, concern is centered in the interference of private transnational agents in political questions of the host country. In fact, it has been shown that on occasion the transnational enterprises have engaged in illegitimate political intervention in the internal affairs of the host countries, which has brought about especially grave consequences in the case of developing countries. This clearly infringes on the national sovereignty of those States. Moreover, as is indicated by a recent study prepared under the auspices of the United Nations, the action of multinational enterprises in the political field may assume less direct and less obvious forms. In the countries of origin, it may be possible for them to influence foreign policy and domestic policy by recourse to their great financial power and to their relations, which are frequently close, with high officials of Government. They may exert pressure in support of or against the Governments of the host countries, according to whether or not they receive especially favourable treatment.

5. There should therefore be proscribed, in absolute terms, the use on the part of the transnational corporations of practices or procedures that involve an action, pressure, coercion, or any political interference in the host country.

C. The transnational corporations shall abstain from interference in relations between the Government of a host country and other States, and from perturbing those relations

6. Experience indicates that, in various circumstances, the transnational corporations have been perturbing elements in relations between countries and have provoked confrontations between those States. Instances are known in which the transnational corporations have requested the Government of a country of origin to intercede before the host Government with

actions of a political and economic nature in support of their private interests. This illegitimate posture has violated, in more than one case, the constitutional provisions of the host country that prohibit the foreign investor from invoking the protection of his Government, given the existence of local recourses for the solution of controversies. The transnational corporations should likewise not exert pressure on the Governments of the countries of origin for the adoption of restrictive measures that may affect the interests of the host countries.

7. The most frequent cause of confrontation between countries of origin and host countries is the circumstances in which the host country nationalizes the properties of a foreign enterprise and the enterprise requests the protection of its Government of origin. The source of the controversy arises from the statement of the case in terms of questioning the validity of the act of nationalization itself or of demanding prompt, adequate and effective indemnity. Naturally, it is a sovereign power of the State to nationalize the property of foreigners or nationals and any argument tending to object to the legitimacy of such measure is not valid. The matter that is subject to resolution is the amount of the indemnity that should be paid and the manner in which this amount should be determined. In this sense, the Charter of Economic Rights and Duties of States sets forth suitable criteria to regulate the subject and to indicate that the State that adopts the measure of nationalization should pay appropriate compensation, provided that all the pertinent circumstances so require it.

8. Likewise, as the charter indicates, when the question of the compensation arouses controversies, this will be resolved in conformity with the legislation and the courts of the State that nationalizes, unless that State should decide to have recourse to other pacific means based on the sovereign equality of States and in accordance with the principle of the free election of methods.

D. The transnational corporations shall not serve as an instrument of the foreign policy of another State or as a means of extending in the host country provisions of the juridical order of the country of origin

9. Cases are known in which countries have seen their exports affected by the extraterritorial application, by the country of origin, of legislation that prohibits trading with certain States.

There likewise exist precedents in subjecting to restriction the movement of capital to enterprises that operate in foreign countries and directives concerning the recovery of financial assets for the purpose of improving the balance of payments of the country of origin have been noted. In other cases, laws and provisions have been applied, principally in the matter of monopolies, that have an extraterritorial effect and that affect indirectly the capacity of the branches in foreign countries to conform to the policies of the host Government.

Another question that is of concern is the fact that the transnational corporations may lend themselves as instruments of foreign policy, including for intelligence activities, contrary to the interests of the host country.

E. The transnational corporations shall be subject to the exercise by the host country of its permanent sovereignty over all its wealth, natural resources and economic activities

10. The natural resources of a country constitute the national heritage of that country and of its people. Practice has shown that the transnational corporations have not always fully abided by the principle that every country, in the exercise of its permanent sovereignty over its natural resources, has the inalienable right to the ownership, effective control and development of those resources. The failure to abide by this principle is a source of concern on the part of the host country.

Whenever the transnational corporations are granted access to a country's resources, their activities shall be carried out in a manner consistent with the priorities and developmental needs as defined by that country.

The transnational corporations must not in any way attempt to obstruct the efforts of the host country to assume its rightful responsibility and exercise effective control over the development and management of its resources.

The transnational corporations, during their presence in the host country, must operate in such a way as to ensure that nationals of the host country can manage and operate the enterprise at all levels, including that of decision-making.

F. The transnational corporations shall be subject to the national policies, objectives and priorities for development, and should contribute positively to carrying them out

11. The intention of this principle is to insist on the necessity that the transnational corporations should adjust their conduct not only to the formal juridical dispositions but that they likewise make their activities subject to the general lines of economic and social policy set forth by the Government of the host country.

12. Special consideration should be given by the transnational corporations to the guidelines relating to foreign trade, finance and movement of capital; financial arrangements and anti-monopoly norms; employment regulations; utilization and training of local personnel; regional dispersion; company administration; transfer of technology and promotion of national technological development; global policy for foreign investment and, in particular, the arrangements for the participation of foreign capital in the diverse sectors of economic activity. Therefore, it is necessary that the affiliates of the transnational corporations adapt their corporate global strategy with a view to satisfying the requirements of the priorities of development established by the host country.

G. The transnational corporations shall supply to the Government of the host country pertinent information about their activities in order to ensure that these activities shall be in accord with the national policies, objectives and priorities of development of the host country

13. The goal sought is for the Governments of the host countries to have sufficient information at their disposal to carry out an effective supervision and regulation of the activities of the transnational corporations. Customarily, because of the lack of disaggregated data, by country and company, the complete evaluation of these activities eludes the Government and renders uncertain the bases for tax, fiscal, credit and other verification. What is sought, in short, is the arrangement of a tangible, acceptable and sure frame of reference that allows for the most exact determination possible of the contribution of the transnational corporation in national development.

H. The transnational corporations shall conduct their operations in a manner that results in a net receipt of financial resources for the host country

14. The fundamental objective is that the transnational corporations contribute to the largest degree possible not only a net initial transfer but a continuing transfer of resources. There is concern that the accounting practices of the companies do not reflect the real flow of the investment of the transnational corporations into the economy, and that scarce internal resources are habitually used to finance transnational corporations' activities, for example, by means of the overvaluation of imported capital goods or the overstatement of liabilities owed abroad.

15. Regarding the balance of payments, it is maintained that the transnational corporations as resident entities in the host country ought to be a source of generation of foreign exchange for that country and a positive force on the balance of payments. The transnational corporations should:

(a) Generate foreign exchange through the exportation of part of the goods and services produced or contribute to the savings of foreign exchange through the substitution of imports;

(b) Pay competitive, international, market-based prices for financial services and technology, not applying transfer prices unless authorized by the Government of the host country;

(c) Respect host country regulations regarding repatriation of capital and remittance of profits.

Regarding point (a), the transnational corporations should not limit their production to the supply of the local market; regarding point (b), the transnational corporations, in their payments for items of financial services and importation of technology, should have a real counterpart and adjust themselves to the conditions prevailing in international markets.

16. The transnational corporations should strictly respect the regulations established by the host country in matters of: repatriation of capital and transfer of profits; external financing; payments abroad for royalties; patents; commercial and financial services; payments to parent companies, affiliates or subsidiaries directly linked or through third persons; and mechanisms for the promotion of exports and defence of the national industry of the host country.

17. There is also concern that the transnational corporations in the host countries may become mere entities for the collection of wealth. There is concern about the acquisition and control by the transnational corporations of national, locally capitalized enterprises through controlled provision of technology, among other means. It is therefore important to strengthen the private or State-owned enterprises so as to maintain an adequate balance between them and the transnational corporations. The transnational corporations should also respect the standards established by the host country regarding forms of capitalization and ownership. In addition there is concern that the investments of transnational corporations will be made with overvalued capital and that those investments, their operation and repatriation will utilize the scarce domestic financial resources of the host country.

18. Following the principle that repatriations and payments made from the host country to other countries by transnational corporations should have real counterparts and not give rise to excessive or unjustified returns, payments made for technology transferred to enterprises in the host countries should not exceed the time in which the technology can be effectively absorbed. The transnational corporations should not charge for technology transferred between subsidiaries and the parent company or between subsidiaries of the same transnational corporation. Similarly, transactions of transnational corporations, with respect to imports as well as exports to and from the receiving country and their subsidiaries, or between subsidiaries of the same transnational corporation and its affiliates, should be made at market prices, avoiding transfer prices unless expressly authorized by the Government of the host country.

I. The transnational corporations shall contribute to the development of the scientific and technological capacity of the host country

19. The transnational corporations should support the local efforts towards technological investigation and development and their consequent diffusion and use. To this end, the local subsidiaries of the transnational corporations should have the facilities and their own budget for investigation and development, encouraging the use of the technologies that take into account the factors of production with which each country is endowed. The Latin American experience shows that the transnational corporations tend to utilize technology imported from the parent company without any adaptation to local conditions, creating various types of distortions. They ought to use techniques that are different from those used by the home company if such techniques

are more suitable for the host country's development. The transnational corporations should not prevent or limit their subsidiaries, affiliates or local companies in the host country from having ample access to world technology.

20. The transnational corporations should encourage the continuing scientific and technical training of the host country nationals, assuring, moreover, their access to executive and management positions.

J. The transnational corporations shall refrain from restrictive business practices

21. There is evidence that the transnational corporations tend to limit their subsidiaries' activities to their respective national markets, through the restriction of exports, control of the means of distribution, supply and external finance. Transnational corporations should refrain from commercial practices such as agreements with competitors for a division of markets or for fixing prices which are detrimental to the receiving country.

The following restrictive practices, *inter alia*, have already been identified:

1. Full or partial export restrictions;
2. Compulsory purchase of products, machinery and equipment from either the suppliers or firms indicated by them;
3. Obligation of entering into a remunerated contract of "transfer of technology" in order to obtain the possibility of acquiring products, machinery and equipment abroad;
4. Imposition of contractual secrecy in an abusive manner, tending to transform a technology not patented in the requiring country, into an industrial property right;
5. Collection of "royalties" on patents which have entered into the public domain or which have not been patented in the home country;
6. Compulsory transfer of improvement and invention rights to the grantor of technology when the improvements have been made by the recipient;
7. Imposition of the use of a foreign trade mark for the acquisition or transfer of the technology;
8. The establishment of sales prices, including export prices;
9. Compulsory export through the technology supplier;
10. Total or partial limitation of production during and/or after the effective period of the technology contract;
11. Maintenance of a contractual vehicle, with or without remuneration, even after the expiration of the industrial property privileges;
12. Imposition of participation in the capital of the firm requiring the technology;
13. Limitation of the research policies and activities of the firm requiring the technology;
14. Obligation of purchasing labour from the supplier;
15. Prevention of contesting the industrial property rights alleged or secured by the technology supplier;
16. Restrictions on obtaining technology from other suppliers;

17. Practices that make it compulsory for the firm requiring the technology to accept additional remunerated technology either not desired or not needed by it;

18. Practices by the supplier which apply quality control or production standards as a means to impose unjustified requirements upon the acquirer of technology;

19. Practices requiring higher payments for technology on goods produced for export than on goods for the domestic market;

20. Submission to foreign courts of information or judgements in lawsuits regarding the interpretation or fulfilment of contracts;

21. Mandatory provisions to be held beyond the life of the contract.

K. The transnational corporations shall respect the socio-cultural identity of the host country

22. The activities of the transnational corporations produce effects in the host country other than of an economic nature that, on occasion, are even more important than the strictly economic. The social institutions, cultural values, traditions, the usages and customs of a nation, are affected by the attempts of the transnational corporations to transplant to the host country their own models of social development that, in more than one case, have differed considerably from the cultural identity and social structure of the host country. That is especially true of developing countries in that the transnational corporation, when importing a culture peculiar to industrialized countries, distorts the local social and cultural character. In essence it is necessary for the transnational corporations to conform not only to formal, legal prescriptions, but also to the political features, usages and customs observed by the host country.

V

General Assembly Resolution 3514 (XXX) of 15 December 1975

Measures against Corrupt Practices of Transnational and Other Corporations, Their Intermediaries and Others Involved

The General Assembly,

Concerned by the corrupt practices of certain transnational and other corporations, their intermediaries and others involved,

Recalling paragraph 4 (g) of the Declaration on the Establishment of a New International Economic Order,[a] which provides for the regulation and supervision of the activities of transnational corporations,

Recalling also the provisions of section V of the Programme of Action on the Establishment of a New International Economic Order[b] emphasizing, *inter alia,* the need to formulate, adopt and implement the code of conduct referred to in the report of the Commission on Transnational Corporations on its first session;[c]

Recalling further the provisions of the Charter of Economic Rights and Duties of States,[d] according to which such corporations should not operate in a manner that violates the laws and regulations of the host countries,

Recalling Economic and Social Council resolutions 1721 (LIII) of 28 July 1972, 1908 (LVII) of 2 August 1974 and 1913 (LVII) of 5 December 1974,

Recalling the report of the Commission on Transnational Corporations on its first session,

---

[a]General Assembly resolution 3201 (S-VI) of 1 May 1974.

[b]General Assembly resolution 3202 (S-VI) of 1 May 1974.

[c]*Official Records of the Economic and Social Council, Fifty-ninth Session, Supplement No. 12.*

[d]General Assembly resolution 3281 (XXIX) of 12 December 1974.

1. *Condemns* all corrupt practices, including bribery, by transnational and other corporations, their intermediaries and others involved, in violation of the laws and regulations of the host countries;

2. *Reaffirms* the right of any State to adopt legislation and to investigate and take appropriate legal action, in accordance with its national laws and regulations, against transnational and other corporations, their intermediaries and others involved for such corrupt practices;

3. *Calls upon* both home and host Governments to take, within their respective national jurisdictions, all necessary measures which they deem appropriate, including legislative measures, to prevent such corrupt practices, and to take consequent measures against the violators;

4. *Calls upon* Governments to collect information on such corrupt practices, as well as on measures taken against such practices, and to exchange information bilaterally and, as appropriate, multilaterally, particularly through the United Nations Centre on Transnational Corporations;

5. *Calls upon* home Governments to co-operate with Governments of the host countries to prevent such corrupt practices, including bribery, and to prosecute, within their national jurisdictions, those who engage in such acts;

6. *Requests* the Economic and Social Council to direct the Commission on Transnational Corporations to include in its programme of work the question of corrupt practices of transnational corporations and to make recommendations on ways and means whereby such corrupt practices may be effectively prevented;

7. *Requests* the Secretary-General to report to the General Assembly at its thirty-first session, through the Economic and Social Council, on the implementation of the present resolution.

VI

Draft United Nations Code of Conduct on Transnational Corporations as of Mid-1989

Note on the Text. Passages in the following text that are enclosed in square brackets were still not agreed among the parties as of mid-1989. The number of such bracketed passages is not, however, a measure of the number of issues outstanding because (a) some of the bracketed passages are *alternatives* to the immediately preceding or following bracketed passages; (b) in many cases passages are bracketed as a consequence of other bracketed passages in the draft code, so that agreements on all such related passages, taken together, are considered to be interdependent. A typical example is the provision on international law: agreement on this one provision would lead quickly to agreements on a number of other provisions.

In many places the wording "should/shall" is used. This reflects the fact that final agreement has not yet been reached on the legal nature of the code. If, as is probable, the code emerges as a voluntary instrument the word "should" will be used throughout. If, however, it is mandatory, the word used will be "shall."

Preamble and Objectives*ᵃ

Definitions and Scope of Application

1. (a) [The term "transnational corporations" as used in this Code means an enterprise, comprising entities in two or more countries, regardless of the legal form and fields of activity of these entities, which operates under a system of decision-making, permitting coherent policies and a common strategy through one or more decision-making centres, in which the entities are so linked, by ownership or otherwise, that one or more of them may be able to exercise a

---

*No final decision regarding the use and contents of headings and subheadings appearing in the text has yet been taken.

significant influence over the activities of others, and, in particular, to share knowledge, resources and responsibilities with the others.]

[The term "transnational corporation" as used in this Code means an enterprise whether of public, private or mixed ownership, comprising entities in two or more countries, regardless of the legal form and fields of activity of these entities, which operates under a system of decision-making, permitting coherent policies and a common strategy through one or more decision-making centres, in which the entities are so linked, by ownership or otherwise, that one or more of them [may be able to] exercise a significant influence over the activities of others, and, in particular, to share knowledge, resources and responsibilities with the others.]

(b) The term "entities" in the Code refers to both parent entities—that is, entities which are the main source of influence over others—and other entities, unless otherwise specified in the Code.

(c) The term "transnational corporation" in the Code refers to the enterprise as a whole or its various entities.

(d) The term "home country" means the country in which the parent entity is located. The term "host country" means a country in which an entity other than the parent entity is located.

(e) The term "country in which a transnational corporation operates" refers to a home or host country in which an entity of a transnational corporation conducts operations.

2. [The Code is universally applicable in, and to this end is open to adoption by, all States.]

[The Code is universally applicable in [home and host countries of transnational corporations] [as defined in paragraph 1 (a)], and to this end is open to adoption by, all States [regardless of their political and economic systems and their level of development].]

[The Code is open to adoption by all States and is applicable in all States where an entity of a transnational corporation conducts operations.]

[The Code is universally applicable to all States regardless of their political and economic systems and their level of development.]

3. [This Code applies to all enterprises as defined in paragraph 1 (a) above.]
[To be placed in paragraph 1 (a).]

[4. The provisions of the Code addressed to transnational corporations reflect good practice for all enterprises. They are not intended to introduce differences of conduct between transnational corporations and domestic enterprises. Wherever the provisions are relevant to both, transnational corporations and domestic enterprises should be subject to the same expectations in regard to their conduct.]

[To be deleted]*

---

*On the grounds, *inter alia*, that the text within the first pair of brackets goes beyond the mandate of the Intergovernmental Working Group on a Code of Conduct.

[5. Any reference in this Code to States, countries or Governments also includes regional groupings of States, to the extent that the provisions of this Code relate to matters within these groupings' own competence, with respect to such competence.]

[To be deleted]

Activities of Transnational Corporations

A. General and political

Respect for national sovereignty and observance of domestic laws, regulations and administrative practices

6. Transnational corporations should/shall respect the national sovereignty of the countries in which they operate and the right of each State to exercise its [full permanent sovereignty] [in accordance with international law] [in accordance with agreements reached by the countries concerned on a bilateral and multilateral basis] over its natural resources [wealth and economic activities] within its territory.

7. [Transnational corporations] [Entities of transnational corporations] [shall/ should observe] [are subject to] the laws, regulations [jurisdiction] and [administrative practices] [explicitly declared administrative practices] of the countries in which they operate. [Entities of transnational corporations are subject to the jurisdiction of the countries in which they operate to the extent required by the national law of these countries.]

8. Transnational corporations should/shall respect the right of each State to regulate and monitor accordingly the activities of their entities operating within its territory.

Adherence to economic goals and development objectives, policies and priorities

9. Transnational corporations shall/should carry on their activities in conformity with the development policies, objectives and priorities set out by the Governments of the countries in which they operate and work seriously towards making a positive contribution to the achievement of such goals at the national and, as appropriate, the regional level, within the framework of regional integration programmes. Transnational corporations shall/should cooperate with the Governments of the countries in which they operate with a view to contributing to the development process and shall/should be responsive to requests for consultation in this respect, thereby establishing mutually beneficial relations with these countries.

10. Transnational corporations shall/should carry out their operations in conformity with relevant intergovernmental co-operative arrangements concluded by countries in which they operate.

Review and renegotiation of contracts

11. Contracts between Governments and transnational corporations should be negotiated and implemented in good faith. In such contracts, especially long-term ones, review or renegotiation clauses should normally be included.

In the absence of such clauses and where there has been a fundamental change of the circumstances on which the contract or agreement was based, transnational corporations, acting in good faith, shall/should co-operate with Governments for the review or renegotiation of such contract or agreement.

Review or renegotiation of such contracts or agreements shall/should be subject to [the laws of the host country] [relevant national laws and international legal principles].

Adherence to socio-cultural objectives and values

12. Transnational corporations should/shall respect the social and cultural objectives, values and traditions of the countries in which they operate. While economic and technological development is normally accompanied by social change, transnational corporations should/shall avoid practices, products or services which cause detrimental effects on cultural patterns and socio-cultural objectives as determined by Governments. For this purpose, transnational corporations should/shall respond positively to requests for consultations from Governments concerned.

Respect for human rights and fundamental freedoms

13. Transnational corporations should/shall respect human rights and fundamental freedoms in the countries in which they operate. In their social and industrial relations, transnational corporations should/shall not discriminate on the basis of race, colour, sex, religion, language, social, national and ethnic origin or political or other opinion. Transnational corporations should/shall conform to government policies designed to extend equality of opportunity and treatment.

Non-collaboration by transnational corporations with racist minority régimes in southern Africa

14. In accordance with the efforts of the international community towards the elimination of *apartheid* in South Africa and its continued illegal occupation of Namibia,

[(a) Transnational corporations shall progessively reduce their business activities and make no further investment in South Africa and immediately cease all business activities in Namibia;

(b) Transnational corporations shall refrain from collaborating directly or indirectly with that régime especially with regard to its racist practices in South Africa and illegal occupation of Namibia to ensure the successful implementation of United Nations resolutions in relation to these two countries.]

[Transnational corporations operating in southern Africa

(a) Should respect the national laws and regulations adopted in pursuance of Security Council decisions concerning southern Africa;

(b) Should within the framework of their business activities engage in appropriate activities with a view to contributing to the elimination of racial discrimination practices under the system of *apartheid.*]

Non-interference in internal political affairs

15. Transnational corporations should/shall not interfere [illegally] in the internal [political] affairs of the countries in which they operate [by resorting to] [They should refrain from any] [subversive and other [illicit]] activities [aimed at] undermining the political and social systems in these countries.

16. Transnational corporations should/shall not engage in activities of a political nature which are not permitted by the laws and established policies and administrative practices of the countries in which they operate.

Non-interference in intergovernmental relations

17. Transnational corporations should/shall not interfere in [any affairs concerning] intergovernmental relations [, which are the sole concern of Governments].

18. Transnational corporations shall/should not request Governments acting on their behalf to take the measures referred to in the second sentence of paragraph 65.

19. With respect to the exhaustion of local remedies, transnational corporations should/shall not request Governments to act on their behalf in any manner inconsistent with paragraph 65.

Abstention from corrupt practices

20. [Transnational corporations shall refrain, in their transactions, from the offering, promising or giving of any payment, gift or other advantage to or for the benefit of a public official as consideration for performing or refraining from the performance of his duties in connection with those transactions.

Transnational corporations shall maintain accurate records of payments made by them, in connection with their transactions, to any public official or intermediary. They shall make available these records to the competent authorities of the countries in which they operate, upon request, for investigations and proceedings concerning those payments.]

[For the purposes of this Code, the principles set out in the International

Agreement on Illicit Payments adopted by the United Nations should apply in the area of abstention from corrupt practices.]*

B. Economic, financial and social

Ownership and control

21. Transnational corporations should/shall make every effort so to allocate their decision-making powers among their entities as to enable them to contribute to the economic and social development of the countries in which they operate.

22. To the extent permitted by national laws, policies and regulations of the country in which it operates, each entity of a transnational corporation should/shall co-operate with the other entities, in accordance with the actual distribution of responsibilities among them and consistent with paragraph 21, so as to enable each entity to meet effectively the requirements established by the laws, policies and regulations of the country in which it operates.

23. Transnational corporations shall/should co-operate with Governments and nationals of the countries in which they operate in the implementation of national objectives for local equity participation and for the effective exercise of control by local partners as determined by equity, contractual terms in non-equity arrangements or the laws of such countries.

24. Transnational corporations should/shall carry out their personnel policies in accordance with the national policies of each of the countries in which they operate which give priority to the employment and promotion of its [adequately qualified] nationals at all levels of management and direction of the affairs of each entity so as to enhance the effective participation of its nationals in the decision-making process.

25. Transnational corporations should/shall contribute to the managerial and technical training of nationals of the countries in which they operate and facilitate their employment at all levels of management of the entities and enterprises as a whole.

Balance of payments and financing[b]

26. Transnational corporations should/shall carry on their operations in conformity with laws and regulations and with full regard to the policy objectives set out by the countries in which they operate, particularly developing countries, relating to balance of payments, financial transactions and other issues dealt with in the subsequent paragraphs of this section.

27. Transnational corporations should/shall respond positively to requests for consultation on their activities from the Governments of the countries in

---

*To be included in one of the substantive introductory parts of the Code.

which they operate, with a view to contributing to the alleviation of pressing problems of balance of payments and finance of such countries.

28. [As required by government regulations and in furtherance of government policies] [Consistent with the purpose, nature and extent of their operations] transnational corporations should/shall contribute to the promotion of exports and the diversification of exports [and imports] in the countries in which they operate and to an increased utilization of goods, services and other resources which are available in these countries.

29. Transnational corporations should/shall be responsive to requests by Governments of the countries in which they operate, particularly developing countries, concerning the phasing over a limited period of time of the repatriation of capital in case of disinvestment or remittances of accumulated profits, when the size and timing of such transfers would cause serious balance-of-payments difficulties for such countries.

30. Transnational corporations should/shall not, contrary to generally accepted financial practices prevailing in the countries in which they operate, engage in short-term financial operations or transfers or defer or advance foreign exchange payments, including intra-corporate payments, in a manner which would increase currency instability and thereby cause serious balance-of-payments difficulties for the countries concerned.

31. Transnational corporations should/shall not impose restrictions on their entities, beyond generally accepted commercial practices prevailing in the countries in which they operate, regarding the transfer of goods, services and funds which would cause serious balance-of-payments difficulties for the countries in which they operate.

32. When having recourse to the money and capital markets of the countries in which they operate, transnational corporations should/shall not, beyond generally accepted financial practices prevailing in such countries, engage in activities which would have a significant adverse impact on the working of local markets, particularly by restricting the availability of funds to other enterprises. When issuing shares with the objective of increasing local equity participation in an entity operating in such a country, or engaging in long-term borrowing in the local market, transnational corporations shall/should consult with the Government of the country concerned upon its request on the effects of such transactions on the local money and capital markets.

Transfer pricing

33. In respect of their intra-corporate transactions, transnational corporations should/shall not use pricing policies that are not based on relevant market prices, or, in the absence of such prices, the arm's length principle, which have the effect of modifying the tax base on which their entities are assessed or of evading exchange control measures [or customs valuation regulations] [or which [contrary to national laws and regulations] adversely affect economic and social conditions] of the countries in which they operate.

Taxation

34. Transnational corporations should/shall not, contrary to the laws and regulations of the countries in which they operate, use their corporate structure and modes of operation, such as the use of intra-corporate pricing which is not based on the arm's length principle, or other means, to modify the tax base on which their entities are assessed.

Competition and restrictive business practices

35. For the purpose of this Code, the relevant provisions of the Set of Multilaterally Agreed Equitable Principles and Rules for the Control of Restrictive Business Practices adopted by the General Assembly in its resolution 35/63 of 5 December 1980 shall/should also apply in the field of restrictive business practices.[c]

Transfer of technology

36. [Transnational corporations shall conform to the transfer of technology laws and regulations of the countries in which they operate. They shall cooperate with the competent authorities of those countries in assessing the impact of international transfers of technology in their economies and consult with them regarding the various technological options which might help those countries, particularly developing countries, to attain their economic and social development.

Transnational corporations in their transfer of technology transactions, including intra-corporate transactions, shall avoid practices which adversely affect the international flow of technology, or otherwise hinder the economic and technological development of countries, particularly developing countries.

Transnational corporations shall contribute to the strengthening of the scientific and technological capacities of developing countries, in accordance with the science and technology policies and priorities of those countries. Transnational corporations shall undertake substantial research and development activities in developing countries and make full use of local resources and personnel in this process.]

[For the purposes of this Code the relevant provisions of the International Code of Conduct on the Transfer of Technology adopted by the General Assembly in its resolution ____ of ____ shall/should apply in the field of transfer of technology.]*

Consumer protection

37. Transnational corporations shall/should carry out their operations, in particular production and marketing, in accordance with national laws, regulations, administrative practices and policies concerning consumer protection of the countries in which they operate. Transnational corporations shall/should

---

*To be included in one of the substantive introductory parts of the Code.

also perform their activities with due regard to relevant international standards, so that they do not cause injury to the health or endanger the safety of consumers or bring about variations in the quality of products in each market which would have detrimental effects on consumers.

38. Transnational corporations shall/should, in respect of the products and services which they produce or market or propose to produce or market in any country, supply to the competent authorities of that country on request or on a regular basis, as specified by these authorities, all relevant information concerning:

Characteristics of these products or services which may be injurious to the health and safety of consumers including experimental uses and related aspects;

Prohibitions, restrictions, warnings and other public regulatory measures imposed in other countries on grounds of health and safety protection on these products or services.

39. Transnational corporations shall/should disclose to the public in the countries in which they operate all appropriate information on the contents and, to the extent known, on possible hazardous effects of the products they produce or market in the countries concerned by means of proper labelling, informative and accurate advertising or other appropriate methods. Packaging of their products should be safe and the contents of the product should not be misrepresented.

40. Transnational corporations shall/should be responsive to requests from Governments of the countries in which they operate and be prepared to co-operate with international organizations in their efforts to develop and promote national and international standards for the protection of the health and safety of consumers and to meet the basic needs of consumers.

Environmental protection

41. Transnational corporations shall/should carry out their activities in accordance with national laws, regulations, administrative practices and policies relating to the preservation of the environment of the countries in which they operate and with due regard to relevant international standards. Transnational corporations shall/should, in performing their activities, take steps to protect the environment and where damaged to [restore it to the extent appropriate and feasible] [rehabilitate it] and should make efforts to develop and apply adequate technologies for this purpose.

42. Transnational corporations shall/should, in respect of the products, processes and services they have introduced or propose to introduce in any country, supply to the competent authorities of that country on request or on a regular basis, as specified by these authorities, all relevant information concerning:

Characteristics of these products, processes and other activities including experimental uses and related aspects which may harm the environment and the measures and costs necessary to avoid or at least to mitigate their harmful effects;

Prohibitions, restrictions, warnings and other public regulatory measures imposed in other countries on grounds of protection of the environment on these products, processes and services.

43. Transnational corporations shall/should be responsive to requests from Governments of the countries in which they operate and be prepared where appropriate to co-operate with international organizations in their efforts to develop and promote national and international standards for the protection of the environment.

C. Disclosure of information

44. Transnational corporations should disclose to the public in the countries in which they operate, by appropriate means of communication, clear, full and comprehensible information on the structure, policies, activities and operations of the transnational corporation as a whole. The information should include financial as well as non-financial items and should be made available on a regular annual basis, normally within six months and in any case not later than 12 months from the end of the financial year of the corporation. In addition, during the financial year, transnational corporations should wherever appropriate make available a semi-annual summary of financial information.

The financial information to be disclosed annually should be provided where appropriate on a consolidated basis, together with suitable explanatory notes and should include, *inter alia*, the following:

(a) A balance sheet;

(b) An income statement, including operating results and sales;

(c) A statement of allocation of net profits or net income;

(d) A statement of the sources and uses of funds;

(e) Significant new long-term capital investment;

(f) Research and development expenditure.

The non-financial information referred to in the first subparagraph should include, *inter alia:*

(a) The structure of the transnational corporation, showing the name and location of the parent company, its main entities, its percentage ownership, direct and indirect, in these entities, including shareholdings between them;

(b) The main activity of its entities;

(c) Employment information including average number of employees;

(d) Accounting policies used in compiling and consolidating the information published;

(e) Policies applied in respect of transfer pricing.

The information provided for the transnational corporation as a whole should as far as practicable be broken down:

By geographical area or country, as appropriate, with regard to the activities of its main entities, sales, operating results, significant new investments and number of employees;

By major line of business as regards sales and significant new investment.

The method of breakdown as well as details of information provided should/ shall be determined by the nature, scale and interrelationships of the transnational corporation's operations, with due regard to their significance for the areas or countries concerned.

The extent, detail and frequency of the information provided should take into account the nature and size of the transnational corporation as a whole, the requirements of confidentiality and effects on the transnational corporation's competitive position as well as the cost involved in producing the information.

The information herein required should, as necessary, be in addition to information required by national laws, regulations and administrative practices of the countries in which transnational corporations operate.

45. Transnational corporations should/shall supply to the competent authorities in each of the countries in which they operate, upon request or on a regular basis as specified by those authorities, and in accordance with national legislation, all information required for legislative and administrative purposes relevant to the activities and policies of their entities in the country concerned.

Transnational corporations should/shall, to the extent permitted by the provisions of the relevant national laws, regulations, administrative practices and policies of the countries concerned, supply to competent authorities in the countries in which they operate information held in other countries needed to enable them to obtain a true and fair view of the operations of the transnational corporation concerned as a whole in so far as the information requested relates to the activities of the entities in the countries seeking such information.

The provisions of paragraph 51 concerning confidentiality shall apply to information supplied under the provisions of this paragraph.

46. With due regard to the relevant provisions of the ILO Tripartite Declaration of Principles concerning Multinational Enterprises and Social Policy and in accordance with national laws, regulations and practices in the field of labour relations, transnational corporations should/shall provide to trade unions or other representatives of employees in their entities in each of the countries in which they operate, by appropriate means of communication, the necessary information on the activities dealt with in this code to enable them to obtain a true and fair view of the performance of the local entity and, where appropriate, the corporation as a whole. Such information should/shall include, where provided for by national law and practices, *inter alia,* prospects or plans for future development having major economic and social effects on the employees concerned.

Procedures for consultation on matters of mutual concern should/shall be worked out by mutual agreement between entities of transnational corporations and trade unions or other representatives of employees in accordance with national law and practice.

Information made available pursuant to the provisions of this paragraph should be subject to appropriate safeguards for confidentiality so that no damage is caused to the parties concerned.

Treatment of Transnational Corporations

A. *General treatment of transnational corporations by the countries in which they operate*

47. States have the right to regulate the entry and establishment of transnational corporations including determining the role that such corporations may play in economic and social development and prohibiting or limiting the extent of their presence in specific sectors.

48. Transnational corporations should receive [fair and] equitable [and non-discriminatory] treatment [under] [in accordance with] the laws, regulations and administrative practices of the countries in which they operate [as well as intergovernmental obligations to which the Governments of these countries have freely subscribed] [consistent with their international obligations] [consistent with international law].

49. Consistent with [national constitutional systems and] national needs to [protect essential/national economic interests,] maintain public order and to protect national security, [and with due regard to provisions of agreements among countries, particularly developing countries,] entities of transnational corporations should be given by the countries in which they operate [the treatment] [treatment no less favourable than that] [appropriate treatment,]* accorded to domestic enterprises under their laws, regulations and administrative practices [when the circumstances in which they operate are similar/identical] [in like situations]. [Transnational corporations should not claim preferential treatment or the incentives and concessions granted to domestic enterprises of the countries in which they operate.] [Such treatment should not necessarily include extension to entities of transnational corporations of incentives and concessions granted to domestic enterprises in order to promote self-reliant development or protect essential economic interests.]**

[50. Endeavouring to assure the clarity and stability of national policies, laws, regulations and administrative practices is of acknowledged importance. Laws, regulations and other measures affecting transnational corporations should be publicly and readily available. Changes in them should be made with proper regard to the legitimate rights and interests of all concerned parties, including transnational corporations.]
    [To be deleted]

---

*In this alternative, the sentence will end here.
**Some delegations preferred not to have a second sentence.

51. Information furnished by transnational corporations to the authorities in each of the countries in which they operate containing [legitimate business secrets] [confidential business information] should be accorded reasonable safeguards normally applicable in the area in which the information is provided, particularly to protect its confidentiality.

[52. In order to achieve the purposes of paragraph 25 relating to managerial and technical training and employment of nationals of the countries in which transnational corporations operate, the transfer of those nationals between the entities of a transnational corporation should, where consistent with the laws and regulations of the countries concerned, be facilitated.]

[To be deleted]

53. Transnational corporations should be able to transfer freely and without restriction all payments relating to their investments such as income from invested capital and the repatriation of this capital when this investment is terminated, and licensing and technical assistance fees and other royalties, without prejudice to the relevant provisions of the "Balance of payments and financing" section of this Code and, in particular, its paragraph 29.]

[To be deleted]

B. Nationalization and compensation

54. [In the exercise of its right to nationalize or expropriate totally or partially the assets of transnational corporations operating in its territory, the State adopting those measures should pay adequate compensation taking into account its own laws and regulations and all the circumstances which the State may deem relevant. When the question of compensation gives rise to controversy or should there be a dispute as to whether a nationalization or expropriation has taken place, it shall be settled under the domestic law of the nationalizing or expropriating State and by its tribunals.]

[In the exercise of their sovereignty, States have the right to nationalize or expropriate foreign-owned property in their territory. Any such taking of property whether direct or indirect, consistent with international law, must be non-discriminatory, for a public purpose, in accordance with due process of law, and not be in violation of specific undertakings to the contrary by contract or other agreement; and be accompanied by the payment of prompt, adequate and effective compensation. Such compensation should correspond to the full value of the property interests taken, on the basis of their fair market value, including going concern value, or where appropriate other internationally accepted methods of valuation, determined apart from any effects on value caused by the expropriatory measure or measures, or the expectation of them. Such compensation payments should be freely convertible and transferable, and should not be subject to any restrictive measures applicable to transfers of payments, income or capital.]

[In the exercise of its sovereignty, a State has the right to nationalize or expropriate totally or partially the assets of transnational corporations in its territory, and appropriate compensation should be paid by the State adopting such measures, in accordance with its own laws and regulations and all the circumstances which the State deems relevant. Relevant international obligations freely undertaken by the States concerned apply.]

[A State has the right to nationalize or expropriate the assets of transnational corporations in its territory against compensation, in accordance with its own laws and regulations and its international obligations.]

C. Jurisdiction

[55.] [Entities of transnational corporations are subject to the jurisdiction of the countries in which they operate.]

[An entity of a transnational corporation operating in a given country is subject to the jurisdiction of such a country] [in respect of its operations in that country.]

[To be deleted]

56. [Disputes between a State and an entity of a transnational corporation operating in its territory are subject to the jurisdiction of the courts and other competent authorities of that State unless amicably settled between the parties.]

[Disputes between a State and an entity of a transnational corporation which are not amicably settled between the parties or resolved in accordance with previously agreed dispute settlement procedures, should be submitted to competent courts or other authorities, or to other agreed means of settlement, such as arbitration.]

[Disputes between States and entities of transnational corporations, which are not amicably settled between the parties, shall/should be submitted to competent national courts or authorities in conformity with the principle of paragraph 7. Where the parties so agree, such disputes may be referred to other mutually acceptable dispute settlement procedures.]

[57. In contracts in which at least one party is an entity of a transnational corporation the parties should be free to choose the applicable law and the form for settlement of disputes, including arbitration, it being understood that such a choice may be limited in its effects by the law of the countries concerned.]

[To be deleted]

58. [States should [use moderation and restraint in order to] [seek to] avoid [undue] encroachment on a jurisdiction more [properly appertaining to, or more] appropriately exercisable, by another State.] Where the exercise of jurisdiction over transnational corporations and their entities by more than one State may lead to conflicts of jurisdiction, States concerned should endeavour to adopt mutually acceptable [principles and procedures, bilaterally or multilaterally, for the avoidance or settlement of such conflicts,] [arrangements] on the basis of respect for [their mutual interests] [the principle of sovereign equality and mutual interests.]

[To be placed in the section on intergovernmental co-operation]

Intergovernmental Co-operation

59. [It is acknowledged] [States agree] that intergovernmental co-operation is essential in accomplishing the objectives of the Code.

60. [States agree that] intergovernmental co-operation should be established or strengthened at the international level and, where appropriate, at the bilateral, regional and interregional levels [with a view to promoting the contribution of transnational corporations to their developmental goals, particularly those of developing countries, while controlling and eliminating their negative effects].*

61. States [agree to] [should] exchange information on the measures they have taken to give effect to the Code and on their experience with the Code.

62. States [agree to] [should] consult on a bilateral or multilateral basis, as appropriate, on matters relating to the Code and its application [in particular on conflicting requirements imposed on transnational corporations by the countries in which they operate and issues of conflicting national jurisdiction] [in particular in relation to conflicting requirements imposed by parent companies on their entities operating in different countries] and with respect to the development of international agreements and arrangements on issues related to the Code.

63. States [agree to] [should] take into consideration the objectives of the Code as reflected in its provisions when negotiating bilateral or multilateral agreements concerning transnational corporations.

64. States [agree not to use] [should not use] transnational corporations as instruments to intervene in the internal or external affairs of other States [and agree to take appropriate action within their jurisdiction to prevent transnational corporations from engaging in activities referred to in paragraph 15 to 17 of this Code].

65. Government action on behalf of a transnational corporation operating in another country should/shall be subject to the principle of exhaustion of local remedies provided in such a country and, when agreed among the Governments concerned, to procedures for dealing with international legal claims. Such action should not in any event amount to the use of any type of coercive measures not consistent with the Charter of the United Nations and the Declaration on Principles of International Law concerning Friendly Relations and Co-operation among States in accordance with the Charter of the United Nations.

---

*It is agreed that the last bracketed text will be deleted provided that the concept embodied therein is referred to in the section on objectives.

Implementation of the Code of Conduct

A. Action at the national level

66. In order to ensure and promote the implementation of the Code at the national level, States shall/should, *inter alia:*

(a) Publicize and disseminate the Code;

(b) Follow the implementation of the Code within their territories;

(c) Report to the United Nations Commission on Transnational Corporations on the action taken at the national level to promote the Code and on the experience gained from its implementation;

(d) Take actions to reflect their support for the Code and take into account the objectives of the Code as reflected in its provisions when introducing, implementing and reviewing laws, regulations and administrative practices on matters dealt with in the Code.

B. International institutional machinery

67. The United Nations Commission on Transnational Corporations shall assume the functions of the international institutional machinery for the implementation of the Code. In this capacity, the Commission shall be open to the participation of all States having accepted the Code. [It may establish the subsidiary bodies and specific procedures it deems necessary for the effective discharge of its functions.] The United Nations Centre on Transnational Corporations shall act as the secretariat to the Commission.

68. The Commission shall act as the focal international body within the United Nations system for all matters related to the Code. It shall establish and maintain close contacts with other United Nations organizations and specialized agencies dealing with matters related to the Code and its implementation with a view to co-ordinating work related to the Code. When matters covered by international agreements or arrangements, specifically referred to in the Code, which have been worked out in other United Nations forums, arise, the Commission shall forward such matters to the competent bodies concerned with such agreements or arrangements.

69. The Commission shall have the following functions:

(a) To discuss at its annual sessions matters related to the Code. If agreed by the Governments engaged in consultations on specific issues related to the Code, the Commission shall facilitate such intergovernmental consultations to the extent possible. [Representatives of trade unions, business, consumer and other relevant groups may express their views on matters related to the Code through the non-governmental organizations represented in the Commission.]

(b) Periodically to assess the implementation of the Code, such assessments being based on reports submitted by Governments and, as appropriate, on documentation from United Nations organizations and specialized agencies performing work relevant to the Code and non-governmental organizations represented in the Commission. The first assessment shall take place not earlier than two years and not later than three years after the adoption of the Code. The second assessment shall take place two years after the first one. The Commission shall determine whether a periodicity of two years is to be maintained or modified for subsequent assessments. The format of assessments shall be determined by the Commission.

[(c) To provide [, upon the request of a Government,] clarification of the provisions of the Code in the light of actual situations in which the applicability and implications of the Code have been the subject of intergovernmental consultations. In clarifying the provisions of the Code, the Commission shall not draw conclusions concerning the conduct of the parties involved in the situation which led to the request for clarification. The clarification is to be restricted to issues illustrated by such a situation. The detailed procedures regarding clarification are to be determined by the Commission.]

[To be deleted]

(d) To report annually to the General Assembly [through the Economic and Social Council] on its activities regarding the implementation of the Code.

(e) To facilitate intergovernmental arrangements or agreements on specific aspects relating to transnational corporations upon request of the Governments concerned.

70. The United Nations Centre on Transnational Corporations shall provide assistance relating to the implementation of the Code, *inter alia*, by collecting, analysing and disseminating information and conducting research and surveys, as required and specified by the Commission.

C. Review procedure

71. The Commission shall make recommendations to the General Assembly [through the Economic and Social Council] for the purpose of reviewing the Code. The first review shall take place no later than six years after the adoption of the Code. The General Assembly shall establish, as appropriate, the modalities for reviewing the Code.*

Notes

ªNo drafting was done on the Preamble and Objectives of the Code. However, the following text was drafted during the discussion on other parts of the Code and the decision was taken to place it in one of the substantive introductory parts of the Code:

"For the purposes of this Code, the principles set out in the Tripartite Declaration of Principles concerning Multinational Enterprises and Social Policy, adopted by the Governing Body of the International Labour Office, should

---

*Further discussion of this provision will take place after related issues, such as the mode of adoption and the legal nature of the code, have been settled.

apply in the field of employment, training, conditions of work and life and industrial relations."

(No decision has yet been taken on the exact location of this paragraph.)

ᵇSome delegations accepted paragraphs 26, 30, 31 and 32 on balance of payments and financing on an *ad referendum* basis.

ᶜThe placement of this paragraph has not yet been decided.

Appendix: Non-Collaboration by Transnational Corporations with Racist Minority Régimes in Southern Africaᵃ

14. In accordance with the efforts of the international community towards the elimination of *apartheid* in South Africa and its illegal occupation of Namibia,

(a) Transnational corporations shall/should refrain from operations and activities supporting and sustaining the racist minority régime of South Africa in maintaining the system of *apartheid* and the illegal occupation of Namibia;

(b) Transnational corporations shall/should engage in appropriate activities within their competence with a view to eliminating racial discrimination and all other aspects of the system of *apartheid*;

(c) Transnational corporations shall/should comply strictly with obligations resulting from Security Council decisions and shall/should fully respect those resulting from all relevant United Nations resolutions;

(d) With regard to investment in Namibia, transnational corporations shall/should comply strictly with obligations resulting from Security Council resolution 283 (1970) and other relevant Security Council decisions and shall/should fully respect those resulting from all relevant United Nations resolutions.

Notes

ᵃThe text of paragraph 14 was agreed *ad referendum* in the working group on paragraph 14, but no final decision thereon was taken by the Commission.

Notes

1   John Kenneth Galbraith, *American Capitalism* (Boston: Houghton Mifflin, 1952), p. 147.

2   Ibid., pp. 147–49.

3   Robert H. Bork, *The Antitrust Paradox* (New York: Basic Books, 1978), p. 7.

4   Ibid., p. 28.

5   Paul A. Samuelson, *Economics*, 9th ed. (New York: McGraw-Hill, 1973), p. 528.

6   Ibid.

7   Richard Hofstadter, "What Happened to the Antitrust Movement?" in *The Paranoid Style in American Politics and Other Essays* (New York: Alfred A. Knopf, 1965), p. 212.

8   Ibid., p. 213.

9   Bork, *The Antitrust Paradox*, p. 406.

10 Galbraith, *American Capitalism*, p. 58.

11 Ibid., p. 173.

12 For a review of international discussion of RBPs during the interwar period, on which the above account is based, see Dale B. Furnish, "A Transnational Approach to Restrictive Business Practices," *International Lawyer* 4, no. 2 (1970): 318–22.

13 William Oualid, *The Social Effects of International Industrial Agreements, The Protection of Workers and Consumers*, submitted to the Preparatory Committee for the International Economic Conference, Geneva. (Printed by Atar, 1926, League of Nations author file B III, Library of Congress, HD 2733.OS.)

14 International Economic Conference at Geneva, 1927, *Final Report*, p. 44 (C.E.I.44.1927.II.46).

15 Ibid., p. 41.

16 St. Benni et al., *General Report on the Economic Aspects of International Industrial Agreements* (E.614.1930.II.41).

17 Economic Committee, *Report to the Council on the Work of the Thirty-Seventh Session* 3–4 (20.1.32).

18 The evolution of the Roosevelt administration's position on antitrust is analyzed in Ellis W. Hawley, *The New Deal and the Problem of Monopoly* (1966).

19 Charles R. Whittlesey, *National Interest and International Cartels* (New York: Macmillan, 1946), pp. 3–4.

20 Sigmund Timberg, "European and American Antitrust Laws—A Comparison," *The Antitrust Bulletin* (1962), p. 136.

21 *Suggested Charter for an International Trade Organization of the United Nations* (U.S. Department of State, September 1946), chapter V, pp. 25–29.

22 Report of the First Session of the Preparatory Committee of the UN Conference on Trade and Employment, London, October 1946, doc. E/PC/T/33, pp. 18–19.

23 Ibid., chapter IV, paras. 2, 3.

24 Ibid., para. 4.

25 United Nations Conference on Trade and Employment, *Final Act and Related Documents* (March 1948), Article 46.1, doc. E/CONF.2/78, p. 35.

26 Ibid., Article 46.3.

27 Public Law no. 165, 82d Cong., 1st Sess., c. 479, 5–6(1951).

28 This change in position has been attributed by a number of observers to the change in the U.S. administration in 1953. See, for example, Sigmund Timberg, "Restrictive Business Practices as an Appropriate Subject for United Nations Action," *The Antitrust Bulletin* (1955), p. 411. Timberg pointed out that "twice within eight years, the United States has led a formidable march up the hill only to beat a retreat and leave its foreign associates stranded at the summit of achievement" (pp. 411–12). It should not, however, be inferred that the Eisenhower administration was less concerned about RBPs than its predecessors. On the contrary, it was precisely in 1955 that the U.S. attorney general's National Committee to Study the Antitrust Laws reported unanimously in favor of the antitrust laws and of the tightening of enforcement of these laws. And, as Richard Hofstadter has pointed out, "The most spectacular and revealing case involving a criminal price conspiracy—the General Electric case—took place during the Eisenhower Administration." This, however, was not inconsistent with a change of position on the usefulness of international action under existing conditions. The proposed UN convention, which required proof of harmful effects before any RBP could be considered illegal, was felt by its opponents to be ineffective as contrasted with the U.S. approach under which many RBPs were held to be illegal per se, and not susceptible to any economic justification.

29 Sweden, E/2612, May 28, 1954; Belgium, E/2612, May 28, 1954: Norway, E/2612/Add. 2, April 4, 1955, pp. 3–4; Federal Republic of Germany, E/2612/Add. 3, April 15, 1955, pp. 3–5; Turkey, Summary Records, 855th Meeting, May 26, 1955, pp. 5–7; Yugoslavia, ibid., pp. 10–13; and India,

Summary Records, 856th Meeting, May 25, 1955, p. 4. Norway, Germany, Turkey, Yugoslavia, and India favored administration of the agreement within the general framework of the General Agreement on Tariffs and Trade (GATT). Compare also the statement of the Netherlands delegation in Summary Records, 855th Meeting, pp. 7–8.

30   Sigmund Timberg, "Restrictive Business Practices as an Appropriate Subject for United Nations Action," p. 423.

31   Ibid., pp. 426–27.

32   GATT, *Basic Instruments and Selected Documents*, seventh supplement, p. 29.

33   Ibid., ninth supplement, p. 28.

34   Argentina, Brazil, Cuba, Egypt, India, Nicaragua, Nigeria, Peru, Tanzania, Yugoslavia.

35   *Proceedings of the United Nations Conference on Trade and Development Second Session*, vol. I, Resolution 25 (II), p. 38.

36   *Proceedings of the United Nations Conference on Trade and Development Third Session*, vol. I, Resolution 73 (III).

37   See the report of the second ad hoc group of experts on RBPS (TD/B/600) submitted to the seventh special session of the Trade and Development Board, March 8, 1976.

38   *Proceedings of the UNCTAD Fourth Session*, vol. I, Resolution 96 (V), pt. 3.

39   See Philippe Brusick, "UN Control of Restrictive Business Practices," *Journal of World Trade Law* 17, no. 4 (July/August 1983). The following discussion is based on this authoritative article.

40   Dale A. Oesterle, "United Nations Conference on Restrictive Business Practices," *Cornell International Law Journal* 14, no. 1 (Winter 1981): 3.

41   Brusick, "UN Control of Restrictive Business Practices," p. 342.

42   Ibid., p. 344.

43   UN General Assembly, Resolution 35/63, December 5, 1980, Section D, para. 3(a), Section E, para. 4.

44   Brusick, "UN Control of Restrictive Business Practices," p. 349.

45   Whether the issue of transfer pricing has been eliminated from the Set may be open to debate since the Set contains provisions condemning not only predatory pricing but also "discriminatory" or "unjustifiably differentiated 'pricing' in transactions between affiliated enterprises which overcharge or undercharge for goods or services purchased or supplied as compared with prices for similar or comparable transactions outside the affiliated enterprises" (Subsection D(4) (b)). However, as Professor Oesterle has pointed out ("United Nations Conference on Restrictive Business Practices," p. 36) the above transfer pricing restriction is subordinated to language that condemns only behavior limiting access to markets or otherwise unduly restraining competition.

46   Oesterle, "United Nations Conference on Restrictive Business Practices," p. 37.

47   Ibid., pp. 38–39.

48 *Report of the United Nations Conference to Review all Aspects of the Set of Multilaterally Agreed Equitable Principles and Rules for the Control of Restrictive Business Practices,* TD/RBP/CONF.2/8, Annex I.

49 Ibid., para. 35.

50 For details see TD/RBP/CONF.2/8, para. 49.

51 TD/RBP/CONF.2/3/Add. 2, Section C.

52 TD/RBP/CONF.2/8 p. 14.

53 See Joel Davidow, "The Implementation of International Antitrust Principles," in *Emerging Standards of International Trade and Investment,* Seymour J. Rubin and Gary Clyde Hufbauer, eds. (Totowa, N.J.: Rowman and Allanheld, 1983), p. 132.

54 Ibid., pp. 135–36.

55 General Assembly Resolution 1314 (XIII), December 12, 1958.

56 Samuel K. B. Asante, "Restructuring Transnational Mineral Agreements," *American Journal of International Law* 73, no.3 (July 1979): 338.

57 Ibid.

58 Ibid., p. 339.

59 This and the following paragraph are based on Samuel K. B. Asante, "International Law and Foreign Investment: A Reappraisal," *International and Comparative Law Quarterly* 37, pt. 3 (July 1988): 588–628.

60 General Assembly Resolution 1803 (XVII), doc. A/5217 (62).

61 The following account draws on an article by Stephen M. Schwebel, assistant legal adviser to the U.S. Department of State, entitled "The Story of the UN's Declaration on Permanent Sovereignty over Natural Resources," *American Bar Association Journal* 49 (May 1963): 463–69.

62 Ibid., p. 466.

63 Letter of December 21, 1962, to Joseph D. Calhoun.

64 Schwebel, "The Story of the UN's Declaration on Permanent Sovereignty over Natural Resources," p. 469.

65 *Proceedings of the United Nations Conference on Trade and Development,* vol. I, Final Act and Report (New York: UN, 1964), Annex A.I.1, p. 18.

66 The countries voting against were Australia, Canada, the United Kingdom, and the United States, while those abstaining included Austria, Belgium, the Federal Republic of Germany, France, Ireland, Italy, Japan, Luxembourg, the Netherlands, New Zealand, and Switzerland. Those voting in favor included Denmark, Finland, Greece, Iceland, Norway, Portugal, Spain, Sweden, and Turkey, together with the overwhelming majority of developing countries as well as the socialist countries of Eastern Europe and China.

67 *Proceedings of the United Nations Conference on Trade and Development,* vol. I, Final Act and Report, Annex A.I.1, p. 309.

68 Banco Nacional de Cuba v. Sabbatino, 376 U.S. 398 (1963).

69 Ibid., p. 428.

70 Banco Nacional de Cuba v. Sabbatino, 390 U.S. 956 (1967).

71 Oscar Schachter, "Compensation for Expropriation," *American Journal of International Law* 78, no. 1 (January 1984).

72 Ibid., p. 123.

73 Ibid.

74 Ibid., p. 124.

75 For evidence on the above settlements, see Richard B. Lillich and Burns H. Weston, *International Claims: Their Settlement by Lump-Sum Agreements* (Charlottesville: University Press of Virginia, 1975). Lillich and Weston examined 75 cases of such settlement.

76 Ibid., p. 125.

77 Ibid., pp. 126–27.

78 Banco Nacional de Cuba v. Chase Manhattan Bank, 658 F.2d 875 (2d Cir. 1981).

79 M. H. Mendelson, "Compensation for Expropriation: The Case Law," *American Journal of International Law* 79 (1985): 414–20.

80 Oscar Schachter, "Compensation Cases—Leading and Misleading," *American Journal of International Law* 79 (1985): 420–22.

81 General Assembly Resolution 3201 (S-VI), May 1, 1974, para. 4. Although this resolution was adopted without a vote, strong reservations about its contents were voiced by the United States, Japan, and members of the European Community. Particular exception was taken to the reference to "permanent sovereignty" on the grounds that in asserting the right of states to nationalize foreign-owned property, the declaration did not include the concomitant duty to pay appropriate compensation in accordance with international law. See discussion of this point below.

82 General Assembly Resolution 3281, 29th session, A/9631 (1974), Article 2. This resolution was adopted by a vote of 120 in favor, 6 (OECD) countries against, and 10 abstentions.

83 Calvo maintained that a sovereign independent state was entitled, under the principle of equality, to freedom from interference in any form, by other states, whether by diplomacy or by force; and that aliens were entitled to no greater rights and privileges than those available to nationals. See Samuel Asante, "International Law/International Obligations and the Code of Conduct" (mimeo).

84 Ibid.

85 Under Rule 83 of the General Assembly, decisions of that body on "important questions" require a two-thirds majority. Substantive issues in the economic field are not, however, included among the "important questions" listed in Rule 83, but Rule 85 provides that decisions to add to the categories of "important questions" may be made by simple majority (A/520/Rev. 15, p. 18).

86 Statement by Ambassador Andrew Young, 63d session of ECOSOC, July 8, 1977.

87 General Assembly Resolution 2087(XX); Annex A/IV/12 of the final act of the 1st session of the UN Conference on Trade and Development and Resolution 33 (II) of the 2d session; and ECOSOC Resolution 1286(XLIII).

88 ECOSOC Resolution 1359(XLV).

89 *Panel on Foreign Investment in Developing Countries*, Amsterdam, February 16–20, 1969, UN Publication, sales no. E.69.II.D.12, pt. 1.

90 *Panel on Foreign Investment in Latin America* (Medellin, Colombia, June 8–11, 1970), UN publication, sales no. E.71.II.A.14.
91 Ibid., pp. 2–4.
92 UN publication, sales no. E.73.II.A.11.
93 UN publication, sales no. E.74.II.A.5.
94 There was general agreement in the Group that the word "enterprise" should be substituted for corporations, and a strong feeling that the word "transnational" would better convey the notion that these firms operate from their home bases across national borders. However, the term "multinational corporations" was used in the Group's report in conformity with the terminology employed in ECOSOC Resolution 1721(LIII). Subsequently, UN bodies adopted the Group's recommendation regarding the use of the word "transnational" but retained the word "corporations."
95 *International Development Strategy: Action Programme of the General Assembly for the Second United Nations Development Decade* (UN publication, sales no. E.71.II.A.2, para. 50).
96 UN publication, sales no. E.74.II.A.5, p. 26.
97 Ibid.
98 Ibid., p. 28.
99 Ibid., p. 29.
100 Ibid.
101 Ibid., p. 30.
102 Ibid., p. 31.
103 Ibid.
104 Ibid.
105 Ibid.
106 Ibid., p. 32.
107 Ibid., p. 105.
108 Ibid., p. 104.
109 General Assembly Resolution 3202(S-VI), May 1, 1974. Although the resolution was adopted without a vote, strong reservations about its contents were voiced by the United States, Japan, and members of the European Community.
110 Department of State Bulletin, September 22, 1975, pp. 432–33.
111 A. A. Fatouros, "The UN Code of Conduct on Transnational Corporations," in *Emerging Standards of International Trade and Investment,* Seymour J. Rubin and Gary Clyde Hufbauer, eds. (Totowa, N.J.: Rowman and Allanheld, 1984), p. 106.
112 *Transnational Corporations in World Development: Trends and Prospects,* ST/CTC/89, p. 353.
113 Ibid., p. 353.
114 Ibid.
115 The governments contributing to the CTC trust fund during the 1970s and early 1980s were Finland, the Netherlands, Norway, Sweden, Switzerland, United Kingdom, Zaire, and Zambia.
116 See Annex VI, paras. 33, 34.

117   Economic and Social Council Official Records: sixty-third session, supplement no. 5, doc. E/5986, p. 13, para. 29.

118   Ibid., para. 33.

119   For further details, see "Experience Gained in Technical Cooperation Activities," UN doc. E/C.10/1988/9.

120   E/5782, para. 6.

121   E/5782, para. 9.

122   Ibid.

123   *The Impact of Multinational Corporations on Development and on International Relations*, UN publication, sales no. E.74.II.A.5, p. 53.

124   Among the more important titles were *Alternative Arrangements for Petroleum Development* (UN publication, sales no. E.82.II.A.22), and *Issues in Negotiating International Loan Agreements with Transnational Banks* (UN publication, sales no. E.83.II.A.18). Other important publications dealt with management contracts, turnkey contracts, engineering and technical assistance consultancy contracts, equipment leasing contracts, arrangements between joint venture partners and various aspects of petroleum arrangements—their main features and trends, financial and fiscal aspects, and natural gas clauses.

125   UN publication, sales no. E.73.II.A.11.

126   The second study was entitled *Transnational Corporations in World Development: A Re-examination*, UN publication, sales no. E.78.II. A.5; the third was entitled *Transnational Corporations in World Development: Third Survey*, UN publication, sales no. E.83.II.A.14; and the fourth was entitled *Transnational Corporations in World Development: Trends and Prospects*, doc. ST/CTC/89.

127   *CTC Reporter* 23 (Spring 1987): 36.

128   E/C.10/1987/7, paras. 2–4.

129   For details of measures taken by member states, see E/C.10/1987/8, paras. 16–42.

130   *Transnational Corporations in South Africa and Namibia: United Nations Public Hearings. Volume I: Reports of the Panel of Eminent Persons and of the Secretary-General*, UN publication, sales no. E.86.II.A.6, p. 14.

131   Ibid., p. 16.

132   Ibid., pp. 20–21.

133   Ibid., p. 22.

134   Problems of competition and monopoly in the pharmaceutical industry were the subject of 73 days of hearings conducted during the 90th and 91st U.S. Congresses, beginning in May 1967, by Senator Gaylord Nelson, chairman of the Subcommittee on Monopoly of the Select Committee on Small Business of the U.S. Senate. A Summary and Analysis prepared by the Congressional Research Service of the Library of Congress was published as a committee print on November 2, 1972. A further summary and analysis of subsequent hearings was published under the same auspices on December 2, 1974. In the United Kingdom a detailed analysis by the Monopolies Commission of the pricing of the drugs librium and

valium led to the conclusion in 1973 that Hoffman-La Roche, the manu-facturer, had set excessively high prices for these drugs, with the result that the U.K. government ordered price reductions of 40 and 25 percent, respectively. Several other European countries took similar action against the same company as well as against other companies with respect to other products.

135   UN publication, sales no. E.83.II.A.14.
136   Ibid., Annex I.
137   E/1983/18/Rev. 1, para. 18.
138   Ibid., para. 19.
139   E/1982/18, para. 143.
140   E/1983/17/Rev. 1, Annex IV, para. 1 (a).
141   E/1984/18, paras. 18–20.
142   E/1986/27 para. 33.
143   E/1987/22, para. 139.
144   ST/CTC/89, p. 39.
145   This section was prepared by Mr. Bruce Harland, acting director of the center.
146   This section was prepared by Dr. Iwona Rummel-Bulska, Chief of the Environmental Law and Machinery Unit of UNEP.

Index

Act-of-state doctrine, 44–45
Ad hoc committees: ECOSOC, 15–19, 34; on RBPS, 15–16, 22–23, 34; UNCTAD, 22–23
Advisory services. *See* Centre on Transnational Corporations
Afghanistan, Permanent Sovereignty Commission role of, 41
Alberta Oil Sands Technology and Research Authority (AOSTRA), 127
Alikhani, A., 58
Allied Chemicals, 132
Amsterdam colloquium on TNCs. (1969), 57–60
ANDI, 60–62
Antarctic, ozone "hole" over, 131
Antitrust laws and policies: efficacy of, 3–4; in European Community, 7–8; first UN initiative in, 1; in France, 7; in Germany, 6–7; in Japan, 6–7; national differences in, 1; postwar, 6–8; purposes of, 2–3; retail organizations and, 2; two-sided nature of, 2–3; in United Kingdom, 7; in United States, 2–4, 5–6; violation of, 3. *See also* Cartels; Restrictive business practices
AOSTRA, 127
Apartheid, 107–13, 156–57, 170
Arm's length principle, 30, 94

Asante, Samuel, x, 38, 174 nn.56–59
Australian Fluorine Chemicals (ATO-CHEM), 132

Balance of payments, TNCs and, 65, 66, 76, 81, 147, 158–59
BAMA, 132
Banco Nacional de Cuba v. Sabbatino, 44–45
Banks: national development, 59; TNCs use of, 84
Belgium, 14, 16
Bell and Howell, 109
Bilateral investment treaties, 76
BING, 132
Bork, Robert H., on antitrust laws, 2, 3
Brazil, 22
Bribery, 56, 151–52, 157–58; resolution on, 99–100
British Aerosol Manufacturers Association (BAMA), 132
Bruce Company, 132
Brusick, Philippe, x, 25, 28
Business agreements. *See* Industrial agreements

Calvo doctrine, 49–50, 175 n.83
Cartels: abuse by, 13; benefits of, 5–6; in copper industry, 20–21; as

About the Author

Sidney Dell is at present a Senior Fellow in the United Nations Institute for Training and Research (UNITAR). He was trained in economics at Oxford and has spent four decades as an economist at the United Nations. He was successively Director of the Division of Financing Related to Trade in the United Nations Conference on Trade and Development (UNCTAD), Assistant Administrator (Programme) in the United Nations Development Programme (UNDP), and, most recently, Executive Director of the United Nations Centre on Transnational Corporations (UNCTC). He has published numerous articles in professional journals and his books include *Trade Blocs and Common Markets, A Latin American Common Market, The Inter-American Development Bank: A Study in Development Financing,* and, jointly with Roger Lawrence, *The Balance of Payments Adjustment Process in Developing Countries.*

Library of Congress Cataloging-in-Publication Data
Dell, Sidney Samuel.
The United Nations and international business / Sidney Dell.
1. International business enterprises—Law and legislation.
2. International economic relation.   3. United Nation.   I. Title.
K1322.D45   1990
341.7'53—dc20   89-27999